DEAD

interesting

Glasnevin Cemetery gravediggers: Tommy Bonass, Tommy Byrne and Benny Gilbert, 1960. *Courtesy of the Glasnevin Trust Collection*

DEAD
interesting

Stories from the Graveyards of Dublin

Shane MacThomáis

MERCIER PRESS
IRISH PUBLISHER – IRISH STORY

M

To my father, Éamonn MacThomáis,
who left for heaven without warning.

MERCIER PRESS

Cork

www.mercierpress.ie

© The Glasnevin Trust, 2012

ISBN: 978 1 85635 805 7

10 9 8 7 6 5 4 3 2 1

A CIP record for this title is available from the British Library

Printed and bound in the EU.

CONTENTS

~: FOREWORD :~

Dr Peter Harbison

It is often quipped that Glasnevin Cemetery is 'the dead centre of Dublin'. But the fact is that there is not one but a number of 'dead centres' of the capital city. In the past, books such as Vivien Igoe's *Dublin Burial Grounds & Graveyards* have been successful in encompassing most or all of them within a single volume. This present volume makes no pretensions to complete coverage. Instead, it takes us on a leisurely – and above all entertaining – stroll through a select number of the city's cemeteries, of which Glasnevin stands pre-eminent as the national necropolis – sacred ground wherein lie the remains of so many famous people who formed and framed the history of Ireland for the last 200 years.

The author is Glasnevin's greatest guide, a man who knows more of the combined history of Glasnevin's dead than anyone alive, and who demonstrates his knowledge with humour and aplomb when he is giving his tours around the cemetery. That same humour, but also appreciation of the human tragedy attached to many of the famous dead who lie there, comes across in the pages of this book. While concentrating on Glasnevin – which he loves best – it also covers other cemeteries within the city's bounds, regardless of creed or politics: Mount Jerome, the Bully's Acre and the Jewish Cemetery among others.

Shane has the ability and the wit to make all of this come alive, and to bring a smile to what many would regard as a doleful subject and to places which most people wouldn't want to be seen dead in! But Glasnevin itself has had a renaissance recently. The vision of two recent chairmen of the Glasnevin Trust – Gavin Caldwell and John Green – the cemetery's CEO, George McCullough, and the horticulturist Philip Ryan and his team, have made the place a joy to walk around, with new paths, restored monuments and well-pruned trees. The impression given is of a place well-cared for and showing honour to the dead, though it is a never-ending job requiring effort and money to show people from home and abroad what a national treasure Glasnevin is – a point most recently underlined by the wonderful new award-winning museum building at the cemetery's entrance.

What makes this book fascinating are the stories that Shane tells about those whose remains lie buried within Glasnevin's towering walls. These are not just about the famous, of which there are obviously many, but also those ordinary folk who never made it into the nation's history books, who may have died from disease or disturbance, from the tragedy of weapons and wounds of war on various continents of the world, or who gave their lives to achieve the liberty which we enjoy – and thank them for – today. The stories range from the heroic to the macabre, from the heart-rending to the humorous – and that, and its great variety, is what makes this book such a lively read. Shane is a master of the tale well told, and he has that rare ability to transmit his enthusiasm to his listeners, a gift which I hope will also be appreciated by the readers of this volume which is issued by the Glasnevin Trust with the wish expressed by reviewers of every good book, namely, that it will have a long and interesting shelf-life.

~: INTRODUCTION :~

Prior to the establishment of Prospect, later Glasnevin Cemetery, Irish Catholics had no cemetery of their own in which to bury their dead, as the repressive Penal Laws of the eighteenth century placed heavy restrictions on the public performance of Catholic services. This situation continued until an incident at a funeral held in Dublin provoked a public outcry when a Protestant sexton reprimanded a Catholic priest for proceeding to perform a limited version of a funeral mass.

The outcry prompted Daniel O'Connell, champion of Catholic rights, to launch a campaign and prepare a legal opinion proving that there was actually no law passed forbidding praying for a dead Catholic in a graveyard. O'Connell pushed for the opening of a burial ground in which both Irish Catholics and Protestants could give their dead dignified burial.

With the passing of the 'Act of Easement of Burial Bill' in 1824, a committee was formed to administer the proposed cemetery. A small plot of land had been acquired for this purpose at Goldenbridge, Dublin, but soon proved insufficient in size. After some investigation a second site, amounting to nine acres, was bought at Glasnevin – to be named Prospect Cemetery. Monsignor Yore consecrated the land in September 1831 and five months later young Michael Carey was the first person to be buried there. The original entrance to the cemetery was located at Prospect Square, but was moved to the Finglas Road in 1879.

On 14 June 1998, at 2.30 p.m., I was wandering around the pathways of Glasnevin Cemetery reading the headstones of countless men and women from Irish history. I had been invited to interview for the position of tour guide by George McCullough. Tired of answering the endless requests from visitors about the graves of the famous, the Dublin Cemeteries Committee had decided to run walking tours. The interview went well and I was offered the position. George had a great sense of how important Glasnevin Cemetery was historically, but this emphasis had been somewhat lost with the day-to-day running of a 170-year-old graveyard.

Over the following years free tours were run and I read every book, journal and newspaper I could get my hands on about death, burial and the people buried within Glasnevin. Often the funerals were recorded as momentous events that captured the zeitgeist, like those of O'Donovan Rossa or Parnell. Yet in the case of the latter, the reports focused on the huge crowds but forgot to mention that Kitty, the woman he had given up his political career for, didn't attend his funeral as she was too distraught to travel. In other cases ordinary Dubliners with equally fascinating tales to tell were buried in anonymity and often unrecorded.

My father Éamonn was a great help to me in my new job as tour guide. He shared every nugget of information he had and pointed me in the right direction, time and time again. He opened his library to me and always had time for my endless questions. Da used to say that for a tour, book or lecture to be of interest, you needed to do four things. One, you needed to tell people something they already know; two, tell them something they don't; three, make them laugh; and four, make them cry.

Da died in 2002 and while standing, heartbroken, amongst the crowd at his funeral, he gave me one last insight. For at his funeral I caught a glimpse of his life that I had never seen while he lived. The gathering of people could be described as nothing short of eclectic. Every shade of politics was present, from the communist reds to the green ultra nationalists. But the divergences were not just in politics. Lollypop women stood beside Trinity professors, while balladeers and newsreaders looked at each other's shoes. It was at that point that I realised that a funeral was, in a way, a short biography of a person's life and that so much could be learned from one. Who was there and why and, often more importantly, who wasn't and why not? From that point on I never lifted a biography without skipping to the last chapter to see what was written about the funeral.

This book is a collection of forty-eight tales that I hope give you an added insight into the lives of the amazing men, women and children who once walked around Dublin – as Mr Joyce calls them, 'the faithful departed'.

Shane MacThomáis

Palm House

9
14
22

16

O'Connell Circle

2

21
5 37

38

Jesuit Plot...

3

17

36
32

27 28
15 25 31
13 23

19

O'Connell Tower

4 30
26
20

7

Finglas Road

Main Entrance

Museum

Airport M50

St Paul's Section

⬇

1, 10, 11, 18, 24 33

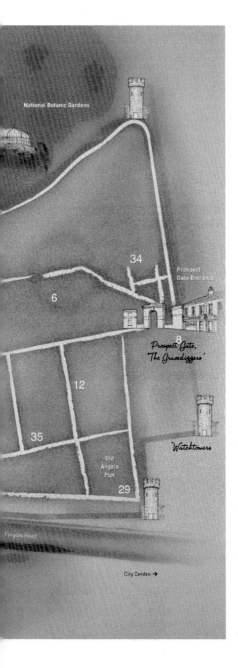

Map of Glasnevin Cemetery showing sites mentioned in the book

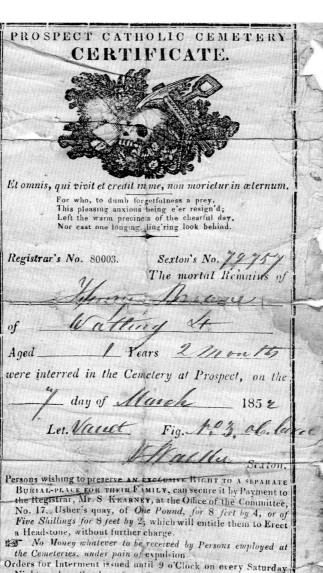

PROSPECT CATHOLIC CEMETERY
CERTIFICATE.

Et omnis, qui vivit et credit in me, non morietur in æternum.

For who, to dumb forgetfulness a prey,
This pleasing anxious being e'er resign'd;
Left the warm precincts of the chearful day,
Nor cast one longing, ling'ring look behind.

Registrar's No. 80003.   Sexton's No. *79757*

The mortal Remains of

Thomas Breeze

of *Watling St*

Aged _____ *1* Years *2 Months*

were interred in the Cemetery at Prospect, on the

7 day of *March* 185*2*

Let. *Vault*   Fig. *No 3, oh. card*

V Waller Sexton.

Persons wishing to preserve AN EXCLUSIVE RIGHT TO A SEPARATE
BURIAL-PLACE FOR THEIR FAMILY, can secure it by Payment to
the Registrar, Mr. S KEARNEY, at the Office of the Committee,
No. 17. Usher's quay, of *One Pound, for 8 feet by 4, or of
Five Shillings for 8 feet by 2*; which will entitle them to Erect
a Headstone, without further charge.
☞ *No Money whatever to be received by Persons employed at
the Cemeteries, under pain of expulsion.*
Orders for Interment issued until 9 o'Clock on every Saturday
Night, and on Sundays. from 8 to 10 o'Clock in the Morning.

CHRISTIE, PRINTER.

Certificate of burial 1852.
Courtesy of the Glasnevin Trust Collection

⌁ THREE CENTURIES OLD ⌁

On 22 February 1832, the coffin of a young boy from Francis Street in Dublin was placed into a small patch of ground on Dublin's north side. From such humble beginnings arose a national cemetery, over 124 acres in size, which became the final resting place of over one million people.

Among Glasnevin Cemetery's residents are some of the people who helped shape Ireland's past and present and many of their graves are cared for almost like shrines. However, the majority of graves are those of ordinary Dubliners, the people who have created this great city, which now spreads out and surrounds their cemetery.

The huge numbers of interments cover a period of immense change and upheaval in Ireland. Such periods throw up great numbers of memorable people. For every poet noted, we may be sure there were another hundred; for every patriot, statesman and scholar, hundreds more; and for every ordinary citizen of Dublin, tens of thousands more. History is a funny thing and sometimes people who have lived hugely historic lives are forgotten in the mists of time.

Of these thousands of ordinary Dubliners, one of my favourites is Margaret Flynn, who lived in 36 Lower Dorset Street. Little is known of Margaret, but she was married to a prison officer, John, who worked in Mountjoy Jail. She died at home of heart failure on 12 January 1911 and was buried in a pauper's grave (OD: 112, the Garden Section).

What makes Margaret one of my favourites is that her record in the cemetery states that she was 112 years old when she died – making Margaret the longest living person buried in Glasnevin Cemetery – and so a record breaker in and of herself!

Margaret was born in 1799, the year George Washington passed away. When she was four years old, the grown-ups around her were speaking in hushed tones of some man called Emmet and his imminent execution. As a Catholic, in her teenage years she suffered the cruel effects of the Penal Laws which prevented her from receiving an education. No doubt she was amongst the huge crowds celebrating the return of Daniel O'Connell when he achieved Catholic emancipation in her thirtieth year.

Margaret was in her forties when famine raged throughout the countryside. And, as the wife of a prison guard, she no doubt heard tell of the desperate thousands committing crimes just so they would be arrested – because at least in prison they would be fed.

The American Civil War ended slavery in Margaret's sixty-fifth year. In her seventies Margaret was reading accounts of Parnell's great speeches and of the Invincibles and their gruesome stabbing of the new under secretary for Ireland in the Phoenix Park.

The biggest funeral ever in Ireland, Parnell's, passed her door in Dorset Street as she undoubtedly looked out the window with her nonagenarian eyes. In her hundredth year, Margaret watched wistfully as a vibrant group of young men and women held protests and gave speeches calling for a new and independent Ireland. Alas, Margaret did not live to see that new Ireland emerge. Yet within her lifetime she witnessed the country move from steam power to electricity, and the Dublin that she knew and loved pass from Georgian grandeur to tenement decay.

Just one life, just one unmarked grave in over a million, but what stories Margaret Flynn – the woman who lived in three centuries – could have told.

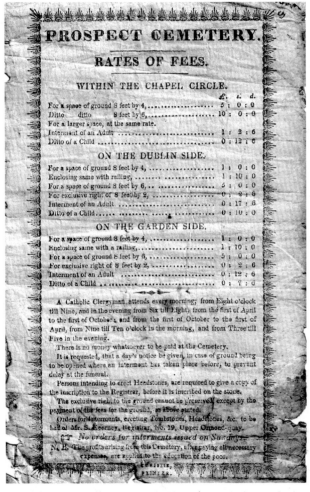

Rates of fees for Prospect (Glasnevin) Cemetery in 1843.
Courtesy of the Glasnevin Trust Collection

~: SEÁN FOSTER :~

Every Easter I spend a few moments thinking about the men and women who made sacrifices during those five days in 1916 when Ireland claimed its place amongst the nations of the world. In the past I have thought of Connolly and Pearse, of Countess Markievicz and Nurse Elizabeth O'Farrell. But on Easters to come, I am going to take a few moments to think about poor little Seán Foster, his mother Catherine and his uncle, Joseph O'Neill.

In April 1916, Catherine Foster was living on Olaf Road in Arbour Hill with her two young sons: Seán, the oldest, and Ted. She had lived there since 1912 with her husband John, who worked for Guinness. On Easter Monday morning, 24 April 1916, she put her two children at either end of a pram and made her way through Stoneybatter and along North King Street. On the way, Mrs Foster met many people all full of chat about shooting across the city. She carried on towards the Church Street junction, where she saw a group of men in the slouch hats of the Volunteers behind a barricade. She immediately recognised her brother, Joseph O'Neill, amongst these men of Ned Daly's 1st Battalion.

True Dub that she was, Catherine started to slag her brother, asking him why he was out playing soldiers at his age. Joseph O'Neill was fully aware of the seriousness of what was transpiring and told her in no uncertain terms that this was no joke and that she had better take herself and her 'childer' home to safety. Catherine didn't believe him at first, but when she saw the look on his face and those of his comrades, she realised that there was more going on than mere games, and hurriedly made her way down Church Street. Nearing Fr Matthew Hall at Nicholas Avenue, she noticed a group of British Lancers approaching from the Bridewell.

Shots rang out from the Lancers first, and then from the Volunteers behind the barricades. Catherine, terrified by the gunfire, ran blindly towards Fr Matthew Hall. As she ran, anxious for the safety of her two babies in the pram, she was caught in the crossfire, and a single bullet struck little Seán Francis Foster under the left ear. As she entered the hall, Catherine was heard to scream, 'They've killed my baby.'

Inside the hall the Rev. George O'Neill, SJ, comforted Catherine and then ran with little Seán draped over his shoulder towards the nearby St Lawrence Hospital. As the priest made his way across the street, the child's uncle watched horrified from the barricade, as his nephew's head bobbed lifelessly on the priest's shoulder. The bullet proved fatal and Seán Foster became the youngest casualty of the rebellion.

The baby's grandfather, Terence O'Neill of Manor Park, was anxious that little Seán should be buried in the family plot in Glasnevin. However, he found it nearly impossible to get permission for the interment since martial law had been declared across the city of Dublin. Eventually, he secured a military pass and on 27 April 1916, Seán Foster became the first victim of the Rising to be buried in Glasnevin Cemetery. He was laid to rest at 7 a.m. that Thursday morning, accompanied by just one mourner, his grandfather. Under martial law only one person was allowed to accompany a coffin to the cemetery. In 1916 this would not have been viewed as a suitable job for a mother and there is every possibility that his father had been arrested since his brother-in-law was out fighting.

Over the next five days 250 men, women and children, all non-combatants who died on Dublin streets, joined Seán in Glasnevin.

A few years ago, I met Terence O'Neill Senior coming back from the grave of little Seán, and he told me the tragic story that you have just read. Seán was Terence's first cousin – his dad Joseph O'Neill was the Volunteer behind the barricade on Church Street.

Seán Foster.
Courtesy of Mary Donnelly

∾ BURIED ALIVE ∾

We have all used the expressions 'dead ringer' and 'saved by the bell'. Well, both these expressions are said to originate from the very real possibility of being buried alive in the nineteenth century. To guard against this many contraptions were invented by coffin makers. The most common and indeed the simplest of these inventions involved a piece of string tied around the corpse's finger running to a bell above ground. Should the unfortunate 'corpse' awaken, then all they had to do was pull on the string to alert the living that all was not well. These 'dead ringers' really were 'saved by the bell'.

When people bumped into these resurrected dead, they usually assumed they were faced with somebody who happened to look like the recently deceased. It would then be explained to them that they were in fact looking at a 'dead ringer'. Over the years the term has evolved to include anyone who bears a close resemblance to somebody else.

Numerous reports of the accidental burial of the living were recorded in the eighteenth century. One tells of Margorie McCall from Lurgan who died and was buried in 1705. Margorie was interred in Shankill graveyard in Belfast. That night grave robbers exhumed her body. They tried in vain to remove a ring from her finger, but could not.

Eventually a blade was produced – with the intention of severing her finger to remove the ring. As soon as blood was drawn Margorie came to – revived from the coma-like state she had fallen into – and scared the bejesus out of the body snatchers. They fled and Margorie climbed out of the coffin and began to make her way home. Her family was gathered around the fireside when they heard a knock at the door. Margorie's husband John exclaimed: 'If your mother were still alive, I'd swear that was her knock.'

And sure enough, upon opening the door, John was confronted by his 'late' wife, dressed in her burial clothes and very much alive. He fainted on the spot.

It is said that Margorie McCall lived for some years after this grotesque event and, when eventually she did die, she was returned to Shankill graveyard. To this day her gravestone still stands. It bears the inscription: 'Margorie McCall, Lived Once, Buried Twice.'

Unknown artist's depiction of a waking corpse.
Taken from a French penny dreadful published in 1881

The nineteenth century saw burials that were even more premature than Marjorie's. Collapse and apparent death were very common during epidemics of plague, cholera and smallpox. Doctors were unwilling to get too close to someone with a very infectious disease and were often a little quick off the mark in pronouncing death.

Some instances would break your heart. In the 1850s, a young girl visiting Edisto Island, South Carolina, died of diphtheria. She was quickly interred in a local family's mausoleum because it was feared the disease might otherwise spread. When one of the family's sons died in the American Civil War some years later, the tomb was re-opened to admit him. A tiny skeleton was found on the floor just behind the door.

Fear of being buried alive – or, to give it its proper name, 'taphophobia' – is still around today. In 1995 a $5,000 casket equipped with 'call-for-help ability and survival kit' went on sale. The casket comes complete with a beeper, as well as a two-way microphone and speaker to enable communication between the occupant and world above. The 'survival kit' includes a torch, a small oxygen tank, a sensor to detect a person's heartbeat, and even a heart stimulator!

∾ FATHER BROWNE ∾

Sometimes it pays to listen to your gaffer, as was the case when Fr Francis Browne was ordered off a ship, en route to New York, by his Jesuit boss.

Fr Browne was born in Cork in 1880. He was educated at the Christian Brothers College, Cork, Belvedere College, Dublin, and the Royal University Dublin (now University College Dublin), where one of his fellow students was James Joyce. Joyce went on to immortalise his classmate as 'Mr Browne, the Jesuit' in the pages of *Finnegans Wake*. At the age of seventeen, along with his brother Willie, Browne set out on a tour of Europe. Armed with a Kodak box camera, he embarked on what was to be his other vocation in life, photography.

When Browne arrived back in Ireland, he entered the Jesuit order and began his noviceship. He spent three years in Italy and returned to Belvedere College where he taught Latin, Greek and English. On 3 April 1912, his Uncle Robert sent him a letter containing a first-class ticket for the first two legs of the maiden voyage of the *Titanic*. The first leg of the voyage took the *Titanic* to Cherbourg in France and the second leg was to Queenstown (Cobh), County Cork. Once aboard Fr Browne photographed the liner, passengers and members of crew, including Captain Edward Smith cutting a lonely figure on the promenade deck. He also took the only photograph of the ship's Marconi room. It was from this room that the fatal word I-C-E-B-E-R-G would be tapped out.

Fr Browne in his chaplain's uniform. *Courtesy of Conor Dodd*

When the *Titanic* reached Cobh, an American millionaire offered to pay for him to stay on the ship for the final leg to New York. Fr Browne eagerly contacted his boss, the Provincial Superior of the Jesuits, to ask if he could stay on board. His reply was a curt, 'Get off that ship.' The young novice duly complied. When news broke that the *Titanic* had sunk, his photographs were published in newspapers across the world, and Fr Browne, the Jesuit snapper, became a household name.

Fr Browne was ordained on 31 July 1915. With the First World War raging, he joined the 1st Battalion of the Irish Guards and served on the front line at the Somme, Ypres and Passchendaele. He was injured on five separate occasions, as well as being gassed, and was awarded the Military Cross and Bar and the Croix de Guerre. His commanding officer, Colonel (later Field-Marshal) Alexander described him as 'the bravest man I have ever met'.

Fr Browne returned to Belvedere College to teach in 1920. In October that same year, when former Belvedere student Kevin Barry was facing execution, Fr Browne cycled to the Vice-Regal Lodge in Dublin's Phoenix Park to make a personal appeal on his behalf. This was during the Irish War of Independence and Barry had been arrested as a member of the IRA taking part in an attack on a British patrol. But alas Browne's appeal was to no avail and the eighteen-year-old student was executed the following morning.

In 1922 Fr Browne was appointed superior of St Francis Xavier's church on Gardiner Street, Dublin. It was at this stage that he began to take his famous photographs of Dublin. By the time he shot his final roll of film in 1957 he had accumulated over 42,000 negatives.

Fr Francis Browne died on 7 July 1960 and his funeral took place on 9 July at the Jesuit plot in Glasnevin Cemetery. With some poignancy, a photograph was taken as they laid this celluloid chronicler of Irish life to rest.

~: FIREMEN :~

My grandfather was a fireman and I have always thought that one of the bravest things someone can do is run into a burning building when everybody else is running out. The Dublin Fire Brigade has been saving Dubliners and their homes since 1862. Unfortunately, one of the earliest disasters to beset the brigade was, in fact, a result of its speedy response to a call out.

At 10.54 p.m. on the night of 5 October 1936, a call to No. 164 Pearse Street was received by Brigade Headquarters on Tara Street. Within two minutes a brand new turntable ladder, the chief officer's car and a pump commanded by Lieutenant Howard arrived to find flames leaping out through the front windows of Exide Batteries Ltd on Pearse Street. Almost immediately upon the arrival of the brigade, a massive explosion rocked the building.

A lack of water pressure made it impossible to fight the fire efficiently at first and the firemen could only look on helplessly at the blazing inferno. The fire eventually spread into a private hotel next door and began to burn towards the railway bridge at the rear. By midnight, the hotel was completely ablaze. However, less than an hour later, with water supplies secured, the blaze was brought under control. But at that point it was noticed that three firemen were missing.

Word soon spread and a search ensued which saw firemen, police and civilians digging through the smouldering rubble. At 4 a.m. they discovered a small piece of hose, a tragic indication of the firemen's fate. Two hours later, the first fireman's body was found, charred beyond recognition.

A second body was discovered an hour later, but it was not until 10 a.m. the next day – after firemen from all over Dublin had arrived to help find their comrade – that the final body was found.

The men who perished were Fireman Peter McArdle, Fireman Robert Malone and Fireman Thomas Nugent. Robert Malone had fought in Boland's Mills during the Rising in 1916, and was later interned in Frongoch in Wales. He had enrolled in the Fire Brigade with his best friend Peter McArdle in the Pembroke Ward of Dublin. Thomas Nugent was the newest recruit of the three, with just four years' service. He left behind a fiancée whom he had been due to marry shortly after the date of the fire. Peter McArdle left behind a wife and seven children.

The families of the firemen accepted the offer of a public funeral and their remains were removed from Sir Patrick Dunn's Hospital. When the cortège reached Pearse Street, it stopped at the site of the fire. Some people were so overcome with grief that they had to be removed from the scene. The procession made its way along Tara Street where the three firemen were each placed on a different fire engine.

Fireman Malone was placed on an engine from Tara Street with twenty men with whom he had served in Boland's Mills forming a guard of honour. The second coffin, with the remains of Fireman McArdle, was placed on a fire engine from Thomas Street and the final coffin, that of Thomas Nugent, rested on a fire engine from Rathmines. Walking behind the engines were the Fire Brigade chief,

Captain Joseph Connolly, Lieutenant James Howard and the families of the deceased, including the seven children of Fireman McArdle. The cortège then made its way slowly to Dublin City Hall.

The bodies lay in state for two days in City Hall, the interior of which had been covered in black draping, with four firemen keeping a guard of honour for the two days.

After a funeral mass said at St Andrew's, Westland Row, the funeral procession made its way to Glasnevin Cemetery, with 170 gardaí lining the route. Fire stations from every county in Ireland were represented, as well as some from Manchester, London and Liverpool. The cortège must have been an image to behold, with hundreds of firemen marching towards the cemetery in their bright red uniforms and shining helmets.

Firemen Nugent, McArdle and Malone. All three perished in the Pearse Street Fire. *Courtesy of the Dublin Fire Brigade Museum*

The floral tributes from home and abroad were so great that a Guinness ten-wheel lorry was used to transport them. An estimated 50,000 people lined the streets. Some women knelt in prayer, many wept openly.

At the cemetery the 'Last Post' was played as the three firemen were buried side by side.

The funeral procession. *Courtesy of the Dublin Fire Brigade Museum*

∼ 1916 MURDER ∼

After the 1916 Rising only two men were tried and convicted of murder. One was Captain J. Bowen Colthurst, who was tried for the killings of five men, found guilty but insane and imprisoned in Broadmoor Criminal Asylum. The other was a Dubliner called Wyatt who was serving in the British army and was convicted of murdering Robert Glaister, an Englishman and an officer in the Royal Navy.

Robert Glaister was born in 1871 in Silloth, Cumberland; he worked as a marine engineer and volunteered for the Royal Naval Volunteer Reserve. With the outbreak of war he was sent to Ireland on board HMS *Colleen*, a clerical centre which was docked in Cobh for the duration of the war.

In April 1916 Glaister was granted home leave and made his way to Dublin to board a ship back to England. By the time he arrived in Dublin the rebellion was in full swing and he had to stay at the Northern Hotel on Amiens Street. Whilst there, Robert Glaister was shot dead.

A general court martial was assembled at Richmond Barracks, Dublin, on Wednesday 14 June 1916 for the trial of Henry Joseph Wyatt, on the charge of having murdered Robert Glaister in Dublin on 28 April 1916. Wyatt pleaded not guilty to all charges before a court of twelve officers and was defended by Second Lieutenant J. P. Coghlan.

William Francis Gray, owner of the Northern Hotel, was the first person to give evidence. He stated that at about 6.30 p.m. on Friday 28 April he was seated, along with some guests, outside the door of his hotel. The accused was on sentry duty in the immediate vicinity. Mr Glaister suggested to Gray that they should stroll down the street, everything at the time being quiet. They had not walked far when the accused challenged them to halt, which they did. He then put his rifle against Glaister's chest. At first Gray thought the man was joking, but as Glaister pushed the weapon aside Wyatt fired, with the result that the bullet went through Glaister's arm. He fell to one knee, but soon recovered, and both Glaister and Gray made their way back to the hotel.

According to Gray, they were making their way up the steps of the hotel when Wyatt fired again, but this time he did not hit either of them. Wyatt pursued them and as they were closing the door he reached them, put his rifle to Glaister's chest and this time shot him dead.

After hearing the evidence of a long list of witnesses, who

SOLDIER ON TRIAL IN DUBLIN

Accused of Murder and Attempted Murder in the Revolt.

DUBLIN, July 14.—Another charge of murder arising from the Irish rebellion was heard today before a court-martial. Private Henry J. Watt of the Irish Lancers was placed on trial for the murder of Robert Glaister and the attempted murder of William F. Grey, proprietor of a Dublin hotel.

Grey testified he and Glaister were walking along the street near the hotel, over which Watt was standing guard, when the latter put a rifle to Glaister's chest and fired. Glaister was able to walk back to the hotel, but as he was entering it, the witness said, Watt again fired, killing him.

The evidence for the defense was that Glaister persisted in passing the sentry who had ordered him back.

A report of the trial. *Courtesy of* The New York Times

all agreed with the evidence given by Gray, Wyatt was given the chance to tell his side of the story. He said that it was about 6.30 p.m. when he was standing about fifteen yards from the Northern Hotel. He claimed that he saw seven or eight persons come out of the hotel, some ladies being among them, and he ordered them to get back. All obeyed the order, except the man in blue, whom Wyatt said he took, at the time, to be a railway official. He told the man several times to 'get back', but he refused, saying that he was a naval man.

Wyatt then stated that he told Glaister that he had his orders to halt, but the naval officer approached further and said, 'Damn your bloody orders, you don't stop me, you're in Ireland not Germany.' Wyatt again challenged him and told him to 'get back', but still he refused. He then said that he fired a shot over him, and the man went back slowly to the steps of the hotel. 'He then called me a clog,' said Wyatt, 'and added, "You don't frighten me. Fire away. If that is all you can do, try another shot."' The accused then said he fired again, on the doorstep.

Replying to questions, Wyatt said that he got a cup of tea from a house in Talbot Street about four o'clock that day, and that, for a time after having drunk it, he felt 'a little strange'.

On Thursday 22 June 1916 the result of the trial was announced:

> Private Henry Joseph Wyatt, 5th Royal Irish Lancers, was tried on the 13th and 14th instant. He was found guilty of the manslaughter of Robert Glaister, an engine room artificer, Royal Navy, and sentenced to penal servitude for five years, which was confirmed by the General Officer Commanding-in-Chief.

Robert Glaister's headstone. *Courtesy of Davis Cleary, Glasnevin Trust Collection*

R. GLAISTER
E.R.A. RNR. 1907SA
H.M.S. "COLLEEN"
28TH APRIL 1916 AGE 45

The body of Robert Glaister was interred in an unmarked grave in Glasnevin Cemetery on 4 May 1916. The grave remained unmarked until 2010 when the Commonwealth War Graves Commission erected a headstone on his grave as part of the Armistice Day (11 November) commemorations.

Henry Joseph Wyatt, having served his time in prison, lived the rest of his life in Dublin as a plumber. He died in 1956 and was buried close to Robert Glaister in Glasnevin Cemetery.

COURTMARTIAL IN DUBLIN.

SHOOTING OF AN NAVAL ARTIFICER.

---◆---

SOLDIER CHARGED WITH MURDER.

A General Courtmartial assembled at Richmond Barracks yesterday for the trial of Henry Joseph Wyatt, a private in the 5th Royal Irish Lancers, attached to the 6th Reserve Regiment of Cavalry, on a charge of having murdered Robert Glaister, an engine-room artificer, in Dublin, on the 28th April. He was also charged with having attempted to murder Wm. Francis Gray, hotel proprietor, at the same time and place, and in a second count with having caused him grievous bodily harm. The accused pleaded not guilty, and was defended by Second Lieut. J. P. Coghlan, Barrister-at-Law.

Major E. C. Kimber, D.S.O., conducted the case for the prosecution.

Major-General Lord Cheylesmore, K.C.V.O., presided over a Court of twelve officers.

Lieut. Norris Goddard, R.N.R., attended on behalf of the Naval authorities.

Wm. Francis Gray, proprietor of the Northern Hotel, Amiens street, stated that about 6.30 p.m. on Friday, April 28th, he was seated along with some guests at his hotel on a seat outside the door. The accused was on sentry in the immediate vicinity. Mr. Glaister proposed to him (witness) that they should stroll down the street, everything being at the time very quiet. They had not proceeded many paces when the accused challenged them to halt. which they did. He put his rifle against Glaister's chest and fired. Witness thought the man was joking, and Glaister pushed the weapon aside, with the result that the charge went through Glaister's arm. He fell on his knee, but soon recovered himself, and witness and the wounded man walked back to the hotel. They were going up the steps when the

Part of a report on the murder in *The Irish Times. Courtesy of* The Irish Times

35

~: GLASNEVIN GHOSTS :~

Glasnevin Cemetery has millions of stories and in some of these the spirits of the dead come to see us to remind us to tell their tales. For example people repeatedly report having seen a ghost or phantom canine around the cemetery. Well that must surely be Captain Boyd's faithful hound.

On the night of Saturday 8 February 1861, the Irish Sea was swept by one of the worst gales of the century. The harbour at Dun Laoghaire was littered with debris and the wreckage of battered vessels. Scores of drowned seamen were found on the shoreline. Among those who attempted to help rescue those in peril was a Captain McNeill Boyd who was in command of the coastguard vessel *Ajax*.

Captain Boyd and three of his men set out in a lifeboat from the *Ajax* to try to rescue sailors clinging to the rocks. As always, the captain's faithful companion, a black Newfoundland dog, accompanied him. While they were on the rocks trying to save the men, the captain and three of his men were swept away by a giant wave. When another lifeboat from the *Ajax* went to search for them, the only living thing they found was the captain's dog, which was still sitting in the captain's lifeboat.

Captain Boyd's body was finally recovered and thousands attended his funeral. The requiem mass was held in St Patrick's Cathedral; afterwards, the funeral procession made its way to Glasnevin Cemetery. The entire time the captain's dog stayed beside his master's coffin. At the cemetery, when the grave was filled in, the captain's devoted companion lay

Glasnevin Cemetery by moonlight.
Courtesy of Philip Ryan

on top and refused to move. He also refused to eat or drink and eventually died of starvation. Many times since then, a black Newfoundland dog has been seen wandering along the paths of Glasnevin Cemetery looking for his master.

But on occasion the explanation is a little more earthly, as in the following tale of ghostly happenings around Glasnevin. During the Second World War, on a dark night in November, a man who worked west of Glasnevin was trudging his way home. It was raining hard and he was soaked to the skin so was relieved when a big, dark car stopped beside him. He jumped in, grateful for the lift, and the car started. He turned to thank the driver and was stunned to see the driver's seat empty. The car proceeded on and the man sat frozen with fear. Suddenly the car stopped and the man's terrified eyes spotted the gates of Glasnevin Cemetery.

Finding the courage to move, the man sprang from the car and sprinted down the road. He turned around after a hundred yards, and to his horror, saw another man about to step into the car. Summoning up all his courage, he turned around and ran back, yelling at the man, 'Don't get into that car, there is something wrong with it.'

The man getting into the car fixed him with a strange stare and said in a grave-like voice, 'I know … I have been pushing it all the way from Finglas!'

∾ FATHER GLEESON ∾

Christians are buried facing the east, except for members of the clergy who are buried facing the west and therefore face their congregation. In Glasnevin Cemetery, St Laurence's section faces the chapel altar in the mortuary chapel.[1] Amongst those buried in this section is Fr Francis Gleeson, who was immortalised in an iconic painting from the First World War.

Francis Gleeson was born on 28 May 1884 in Templemore, County Tipperary. One of thirteen children, he showed early signs of intelligence and embarked on a vocation to the priesthood upon leaving school. At the outbreak of the First World War in 1914, Fr Gleeson volunteered as a military chaplain. He was quickly sent to France and found himself attached to the 2nd Battalion of the Royal Munster Fusiliers.

As an officer, Gleeson had volunteered for a year of service and he spent all of his time with the Munsters. They saw service in Belgium and Northern France. You get a brief glimpse into the character of Fr Gleeson from Robert Graves' 1929 book *Good-bye to All That*:

> Jovial Fr Gleeson of the Munsters, when all the officers were killed or wounded at the first battle of Ypres, had stripped off his black badges and, taking command of the survivors, held the line.

---

1   Five areas of the cemetery are named after saints. St Laurence's section is named after St Laurence O'Toole, first Irish-born archbishop of Dublin. The other sections are St Paul's, St Brigid's, St Mobhi's and St Patrick's.

In May 1915 Gleeson and his battalion took part in the Battle of Aubers Ridge. The battalion moved forward to the trenches on 8 May 1915 and at Rue du Bois they halted near a wayside shrine. Fr Gleeson on horseback, facing the battalion, gave them a general absolution. The famous war illustrator Fortunino Matania later captured the scene in paint.

At 5.30 a.m. the next morning, the British attack began. Leaving their trenches the men barely made it a few yards before they were cut down by machine-gun fire. Those who were not killed, lay wounded in no-man's-land, unable to move. Fr Gleeson comforted those he could and administered the last rites. He described it in his war diary:

> Spent all night trying to comfort, aid and remove the wounded. It was ghastly to see them lying there in the cold, cheerless outhouses, on bare stretchers with no blankets to cover their freezing limbs.

The attack was a complete disaster; the British had under-estimated the strength of German defences and thousands were killed as the German army mowed down the neat rows of attacking soldiers. The 2nd Battalion of the Royal Munster Fusiliers lost a huge number of men: over nineteen officers and 370 other ranks were reported dead in less than two hours. The total of British killed and wounded was approximately 11,000 in one morning.

Fr Gleeson returned home in September 1915, having seen his battalion decimated over the course of a year. This had taken a terrible toll on him, and on leaving he wrote:

I am sorry to be leaving the dear old Munster lads, but I really can't stand it any longer. I do not like the life, though I love the poor men ever so much.

Back in Dublin he became a curate in the Church of Our Lady of Lourdes, Gloucester Street. But a year later he expressed his wish to return to his old battalion and he volunteered for two years' service with the army. He remained with the Munsters until the end of the war.

Fr Gleeson spent the rest of his life in Ireland serving as a chaplain for a time with the Irish Free State army and in Aughrim and Meath Streets, and also Bray. He was elected to be a member of the Metropolitan Chapter, with the title of canon, on 7 May 1956. He died on 26 June 1959.

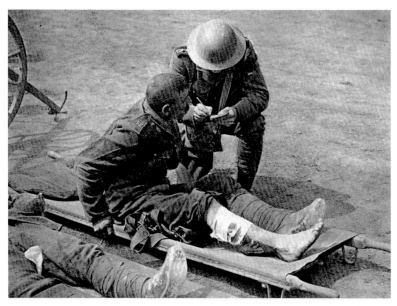

Fr Gleeson writing a letter for a wounded soldier. *Courtesy of Conor Dodd*

~ THE GRAVEDIGGERS ~

On 22 February 1832, John O'Neill, owner of the Prince of Wales Hotel on the North Wall, looked out the window of his family residence at No. 1 Prospect Square and watched as the coffin of a little boy from the Liberties was buried in the adjoining field. What he witnessed that day was the first burial in what was to become Glasnevin Cemetery. John was a shrewd businessman and realised that funerals meant people, and people got thirsty. One year later he converted part of his home into a pub. Both the pub and the cemetery became famous Dublin landmarks.

Initially relations between pub and cemetery were cordial. When the cemetery's founder, Daniel O'Connell, secured a new road bypassing a local toll, the pub responded by stocking 'O'Connell Ale' brewed by O'Connell's youngest son, Daniel Jr, in his James' Street brewery.

In 1836, however, the cemetery committee made a rule that, 'No interment is permitted to take place in either of the cemeteries after 12 o'clock (noon), except of bodies brought from or beyond a distance of seven miles from the General Post Office, Dublin.'

The chief reason for this new rule was the growing number of complaints that mourners attending afternoon funerals were becoming 'increasingly rowdy and clearly intoxicated'. Things came to a head in January 1836 when the cemetery's caretaker, Mr Reynolds, found two unaccompanied coffins lying outside its gates, whilst the mourners took a break from their solemn duty in the adjacent pub.

John O'Neill was licensee of the pub until 1835, when he signed over the business to John Kavanagh on his marriage to his daughter Suzanne. At this point the pub was officially registered and given the name of its new owner, which it retains to this day. John and Suzanne had twenty-five children, three of whom served in the Union Army in the American Civil War and were mentioned for bravery after the Battle of Gettysburg. One of these, Joseph, returned to Ireland in 1877 and became the pub's new licensee.

Two years later, however, the business suffered a setback when the original cemetery gates were closed and a new entrance was opened on the Finglas Road. From then on most funeral business tended to go to Hedigan's on Prospect Road, another old Dublin pub that features in the 'Hades' chapter of James Joyce's *Ulysses*.

The closing of the gate in 1879 witnessed the start of a new custom. Digging graves is thirsty work and it had been a habit of the workmen from the cemetery to sample Kavanagh's wares during their hours of work for the cemetery board. Many a raid was done by the foreman on the premises

Kavanagh's pub today. *Courtesy of the Glasnevin Trust Collection*

An advertisement for Kavanagh's pub from the 1890s.
Courtesy of the Glasnevin Trust Collection

to make sure the men did their drinking in their own time. With the closing of the Prospect Square gate in 1879, the diggers could no longer easily pop out for their jars, so they would simply knock with their shovels on the wall of the pub. The Kavanagh's would then pass drinks through the bars of the gate. This was a risky practice, for if the men were caught drinking on duty they would be sacked.

By the early twentieth century up to fifty gravediggers and groundsmen were employed in the cemetery, and Kavanagh's was firmly established as their local. As they clocked off from a hard day's digging, creamy pints would be set up on the counter, earning the pub its unofficial name – 'The Gravediggers'. This unique Dublin pub has attracted thousands of punters over the last 176 years – even Salvatore Schillaci, the famous Italian footballer, enjoyed a pint at Kavanagh's bar while filming his advert for Smithwicks.

~: GUNNING AND THE ARMY PAY CORPS :~

Nothing gets past the Army Pay Corps. In 1916 when they got news that an old soldier was in prison for a month they stopped his pension, saving them a pound. The soldier's name was Michael Gunning

Gunning enlisted in the Royal Irish Regiment under the name Michael Lawless from Turner Cottages, Ballsbridge, on 8 July 1901 for seven years' service. Why he used the name Lawless to enlist is unclear. On the day he enlisted, his army papers describe him as being eighteen years of age and five feet three inches tall. He had brown hair, a fresh complexion and brown grey eyes. His distinctive marks included a few scars and a smiling face tattooed on his forearm.

He served in Ireland until he was posted to South Africa on 17 December 1902. During his service in Africa he fought against the Zulus in the Bambatha Rebellion in Natal in 1906 and received the very rare Natal Medal. He remained in South Africa until being posted to India in 1910.

During his early service Michael was never far from trouble with his superior officers. He was court-martialled three times for being absent without leave and received a number of detention sentences. Although he never rose above the rank of private, his commanding officer still described him as a good soldier in his army papers.

At the outbreak of the First World War, Michael re-turned home and was sent to France as part of the British Expeditionary Force on 19 December 1914 with the 1st Battalion of the Royal Irish Regiment. His regiment saw

A veteran soldier of the Royal Irish Regiment with South African medals.
Courtesy of the Glasnevin Trust Collection

Soldiers in South Africa. *Courtesy of Conor Dodd*

service at some of the most horrific and dangerous battles of the First World War, including Mons, Le Cateau, Marne, Aisne, La Bassée and Ypres. In action with the Royal Irish Regiment at Ypres on 20 April 1915, Gunning was shot through the back, with the bullet exiting just below his right nipple. He was immediately paralysed in the lower legs. Having been declared totally incapacitated, he was discharged from military service on 6 December 1915 and returned to Dublin.

On 15 July 1916 he was arrested for assault by the Dublin Metropolitan Police and sentenced to one month's imprisonment. The army pay corps heard of his arrest. They immediately sent him a letter stating that, while he was incarcerated, he would forfeit his army pension for the length of his stay in jail. In what looks like a case of bureaucratic inefficiency, it took until 27 December 1916 for the corps to reinstate Gunning's pension.

Diagnosed as having tuberculosis in December 1917, Gunning was sent to Our Lady of Lourdes Hospital, Kingstown (Dun Laoghaire), where he died on 20 September 1918 at thirty-five years of age. His address at the time of his death was 14 Thorncastle Street, Ringsend, Dublin. He was buried in MJ 307, St Bridget's Section, in an unpurchased plot.[2]

Michael Gunning was awarded two medals for his service in the First World War, the British War Medal and the Victory Medal.

---

2   What is described as an unpurchased plot is in effect a pauper's grave. Up to twenty-four people would be buried in the grave until it was considered full. The grave would never have a headstone as the committee, not the deceased, owned the grave.

∽ FINGLAS GRAVEYARD ∾

The next time you're having a hectic time in Finglas Village why not pop into St Canice's Graveyard – a real oasis of calm – and take a few quiet moments to reflect on the area's past? To enter the graveyard call into the last house on the laneway where the caretaker will grant you access. The graveyard is also open all day Sunday.

Finglas is an ancient place. It first appears in history in *The Annals of the Four Masters* as the site of an abbey linked with St Canice, who died in AD 598. According to legend, the ground on which the abbey stood was chosen and sanctified by St Patrick himself. Our patron saint is said to have prophesied that 'a great town will arise at the ford of hurdles in the valley beneath'.

Canice travelled from his home in what is now County Derry to Dublin to attend the monastic school founded by St Mobhi on the banks of the Tolka at Glasnevin. Here he made friends with another Ulsterman, Colmcille, the son of a king. Having completed their studies at Glasnevin, the two young men were ordained. Colmcille went to Swords to found a monastery, while Canice crossed the Tolka and made his way to the remote village of Finglas, where he founded a monastery and a school.

There are over 1,000 people buried in St Canice's Graveyard. The earliest gravestone – for the Ryves family – is dated 1647. However, people were buried in the graveyard long before that. Both Protestants and Catholics were interred here, but their funerals came in through different gates.

The Nethercross, Finglas Graveyard. *Author's collection*

The graveyard's most famous resident is probably Eliza Wollstonecraft-Bishop. Eliza was born in London in 1764 and was the sister of Mary Wollstonecraft, the eighteenth-century writer, philosopher and feminist. Mary is best known for her work *A Vindication of the Rights of Woman*, the feminist bible, as well as for being the mother of Mary Shelley, author of the horror novel *Frankenstein*.

The cemetery is probably best known for the Nethercross, which the monks of St Canice's Abbey erected in the tenth century. The Barony of Nethercross, which spread from Finglas to beyond Ballymun, gets its name from this cross. Composed of granite, it has a circular top with spiral carvings, and originally depicted scenes from the bible. Unfortunately these carvings have been worn away by time.

The Nethercross was originally erected in the grounds of an abbey beside Brookfield Avenue (just north of Mellowes Road), and stood there for centuries, until the people of Finglas heard of Cromwell's landing at Ringsend in August 1649. They immediately dismantled the cross, fearful that the invading army would destroy it as a piece of Catholic imagery. Its parts were buried in the cemetery and made to look like a freshly cut grave in order to fool Cromwell's soldiery.

The cross remained hidden for the next 160 years until the dedication of one man was to lead to it being erected once more. Robert Walsh, in his book *Fingal and its Churches* tells how his grandfather, Rev. Robert Walsh, became curate of the parish in 1806. He was a man of literary and antiquarian pursuits and it was not long before he went out and talked to the good people of Finglas and heard their tales of ancient happenings. The reverend resolved to try to find this buried cross. He tracked down an old man who told him a family story as handed down to him by his father. One of his ancestors, as a boy, had been present at the burial of the cross in a corner of one of the Glebe fields.

Dr Walsh proceeded, with some workmen, to the exact spot indicated in the old man's account. Here he unearthed the cross from its hiding place, and had it erected in the south-east corner of the ancient graveyard, where it still stands today.

This tiny graveyard has had no new plots since 1955 and today people can only be buried there if they have an existing family grave.

~: HUGUENOTS :~

'He's as honest as a Huguenot', is an old Dublin expression that is little used now, but you only need to look at a Dublin street map to see that this community had a profound effect on Dublin in the eighteenth century.

One of their burial places is a small oasis of quiet in the heart of the Hibernian metropolis and is the oldest non-conformist cemetery in Europe. The graveyard is located near St Stephen's Green, just a stone's throw from the Shelbourne Hotel. Although often described as being 'on the Green', it is actually on the north side on Merrion Row, a small street linking St Stephen's Green with Baggot Street.

The Huguenots, Protestants and followers of John Calvin, fled France in their thousands following religious persecution initiated around 1661 by Louis XIV. The name Huguenot is believed to be derived from St Hugo, a Protestant at the time of the Reformation, although other origins have been suggested. Persecution of Protestants had been going on in France sporadically since the middle of the sixteenth century. For example, on 24 August 1572, the Massacre of St Bartholomew's Day witnessed the slaughter of thousands. By 1662 the number of Protestants in France had grown to over one million; in 1685 Louis XIV revoked the Edict of Nantes (which had given French Protestants substantial rights) and made Protestantism illegal, with the result that more than 400,000 fled the country. In fact the word 'refugee' originated with them, taken from the French word *réfugié*, meaning to have taken shelter.

The Huguenot exiles were encouraged to come to Ireland by James Butler, Viceroy and 1st Duke of Ormonde, who had spent twelve years in exile in France after the Irish and Royalist forces were defeated by Oliver Cromwell. Ormonde had encountered Huguenots in Paris and Normandy, and hoped that their skills and capital could help stimulate the Irish economy and introduce new industries.

In Dublin they settled in the Liberties, bringing with them their skills and traditions. Their word was their bond and the saying 'as honest as a Huguenot' testified to their integrity. Their success in weaving woollen goods and flooding the market with high-class products resulted in the English parliament banning the export of woollen goods entirely – thus incurring the 'savage indignation' of Dean Swift at this cruel blow to Ireland's prosperity.

Like most exiled communities, the Huguenots in Ireland tried to maintain their traditions and language, but as time went on they became increasingly integrated into the population and their language withered, its last speakers dying out in the early 1800s.

In 1693 the brewer Peter Ward leased Plot No. 10 on Merrion Row to the Huguenots for the princely sum of £16 and it became the designated 'French Burial Ground' for Dublin's small community of Huguenot refugees. This little cemetery has only one path and is planted with bluebells which flower each spring. There are only thirty-six headstones, but it is known that 240 families are buried there. Traditionally Calvinists refrain from marking graves with headstones. Over the gateway are the words 'Huguenot Cemetery 1693', but this isn't the original location of the entrance as Dublin Corporation moved it back four feet in 1936.

The burial ground, which belongs to the French Huguenot Fund, was restored in 1988 and reopened by the French ambassador in November 1990. Alas the cemetery is not open to visitors, though it is visible through the railings and a list of 239 surnames of those buried is inscribed on the wall plaque to the left. These include Becquett (ancestors of Samuel Beckett) and D'Olier, who gave his name to the Dublin street.

The next time you are walking along Merrion Row, stick your head through the railings and spare a thought for the honest citizens – the Huguenots – who found refuge in Dublin over 300 years ago.

The Huguenot Cemetery on Merrion Row. *Courtesy of Gary McMurray*

⁓ JEWISH CEMETERY ⁓

The next time you're walking along Fairview Strand, look out for a plaque on the side of a house that states: 'Built in the year 5618'. No, it's not a house from the future or a stone cutter slightly the worse for wear, but a sign that you are outside one of the oldest cemeteries in Dublin.

The land was first leased on 28 October 1718 on behalf of the Ashkenazim (Jews descended from the medieval Jewish communities of the west of Germany) to give the local Jewish community on Philipsburg Avenue a burial place of their own. The plot, measuring just 2,500 square metres, was a place of burial for the Jews of Dublin up to 1900, when the current cemetery in Dolphin's Barn opened.

One of the last burials to take place in the Fairview Strand Cemetery, also know as Ballybough Cemetery, was in 1908. Lewis Harris was elected an alderman of the City of Dublin. Tragically, the day before he was to be made lord mayor, he died. He was buried in Fairview beside his wife Juliette.

Initially the burial ground in Fairview was rented for a period of forty years, but in 1746 its officials were threatened with prosecution for the recovery of rent arrears. Assistance was sought from the Spanish-Portuguese Synagogue in London who suggested the plot be bought. The transaction took place on 17 September 1748 naming Michael Phillips of Crane Lane, Dublin, as the leaseholder for 1,000 years at the annual rent of one peppercorn.

In 1857 a stone wall and the gate lodge were added to

The Jewish Cemetery and the plaque on the house beside it recording the year of its construction. *Author's Collection*

the plot and on completion observant Dubliners may have been confused with the bizarrely dated inscription 'built in the year 5618' on the plaque on the gate lodge. Those familiar with the Jewish calendar, however, would have known that 5618 represents 1857. The Jewish calendar is based on the lunar month, with names for each month dating back to the Babylonian captivity of the Jews in 3760 BC.

The cemetery fell prey to thieves over the years – at first for the bodies and latterly for the marble headstones, which could be remodelled into saleable items. An old Dublin yarn tells of the disappearance of the headstone of one Solomon Cohen. Upon visiting a Christian friend in the area, one of his sons remarked how his father appeared to have found his final resting place in his friend's fireplace.

Today 148 tombstones still stand in this little gem of a cemetery. They are inscribed in Hebrew and English, with the Jewish calendar month of death followed by the birth, age and place of origin of the person. The oldest surviving stone is that of Joseph Wills – or 'Jacob Frenchman' to his friends – dated 1777.

Access to the cemetery can be gained from the caretakers who live in the house (the old gate lodge). At the time of writing they are the charming Mr and Mrs O'Neill. Simply call them to make an appointment.

∽ LIAM WHELAN ∾

Eighteen boys dressed in the blue and white hoops of their club colours lifted the coffin from the Dakota aeroplane, and with their studs tapping a footballer's tattoo, carried it towards an airport building while thousands of Dubliners watched in silence. Their player had returned home.

William Augustine Whelan was born in Cabra, Dublin, on 1 April 1935. Also called Billy, he was best known as Liam, and came from a large, devout Roman Catholic family who lived on Attracta Road in Cabra. His father John died in 1943 when Liam was just eight years old.

Liam began his football career playing for the Dublin club Home Farm. Whelan's talent and skill were quickly spotted and Manchester United Football Club signed him in 1953 when he was eighteen. There was an early indicator of just how talented Liam was when, on a youth team trip to Switzerland in 1954, the Brazilian World Cup team stopped to watch the young team play and were so impressed with Liam that they wanted to take him back to Brazil!

Liam Whelan made his debut in the Manchester United first team in 1955. He made ninety-eight appearances as inside forward from then until 1958, scoring fifty-two goals. The team, under their manager Matt Busby, had won back-to-back league titles in 1956 and 1957 when Whelan was their top scorer, with an astonishing twenty-six goals in thirty-nine appearances. This group of gifted and youthful players became known as the 'Busby Babes'.

Liam Whelan made his international debut for Ireland on

10 May 1956 against Holland, and the Irish team won 4–1. He also played for the national team against Denmark in the same year and in two matches against England in May 1957.

On 6 February 1958, the Manchester United team was returning from a European Cup match in Belgrade. The plane had stopped to refuel in Munich. It was a snowy night and, as it attempted its third take-off, British European Airways Flight 609 crashed. Of the forty-four people on board, twenty were killed instantly, including eight of Busby's Babes: Roger Byrne, Eddie Colman, Tommy Taylor, David Pegg, Geoff Bent, Mark Jones, Duncan Edwards and Liam Whelan. In the moments leading up to the crash, it is reported that Liam Whelan, a devout Roman Catholic, said, 'If the worst happens, I am ready for death … I hope we all are …' He was just twenty-two years old.

On Wednesday 12 February 1958, the coffin of young Liam left Dublin airport for the Church of Christ the King in Cabra. His mother Elizabeth, brothers Christy and John, and sisters Alice, Rita and Maura sat in the family car with his fiancée, Ruby McCullough, whom he had planned to marry in June. Thousands lined the route, as a guard of honour of players from Home Farm marched beside the hearse. Representatives of all the football clubs in Ireland were present and the Irish Taxi Owners Association placed twenty free cars at the family's disposal.

At the packed church, many who could not gain entrance remained in the car park and gardaí had to clear the way for the cortège to make its way to Glasnevin Cemetery. At the cemetery RAF chaplain Rev. C. Mulholland, a friend of Liam's, officiated at the grave.

On 8 December 2006 the railway bridge on Faussagh Road, Cabra, was renamed 'Liam Whelan Bridge'. At the ceremony, Bobby Charlton, a team-mate of Liam's said:

> Billy had brilliant close control and was a natural goal scorer. His forte was to scheme, to shape possibilities with his skill and excellent vision. [He] scored so many goals from midfield he would be a wonder of today's game.

Liam Whelan's grave. *Courtesy of David Cleary, Glasnevin Trust Collection*

~: THE LOCKOUT :~

James Larkin said: 'The great appear great because we are on our knees: Let us rise.'

The picket lines of today continue a tradition amongst Dublin workers, who have spent thousands of days over the last 100 years heeding Larkin's call. Some, like James Nolan, paid with their lives for being in a trade union.

In 1913 the conditions for Dublin workers were appalling. Thousands worked a seventy-hour week for less than £1, and women's wages could be less than half of that. It was no wonder then that the Irish Transport and General Workers' Union (ITGWU) under 'Big' Jim Larkin had grown to 10,000 members by 1913.

The bosses, catching wind of the workers' mood, had begun to prepare for trouble by banding together in the Dublin Employers' Federation. Their leader was William Martin Murphy, owner of the Irish Independent Press Group and the Dublin Tramways Company.

On 21 August 1913, 200 workers in the parcels' office of the Tramway Company received the following notice:

> As the directors understand that you are a member of the Irish Transport Union, whose methods are disorganising the trade and business of the city, they do not further require your services. The parcels traffic will be temporarily suspended. If you are not a member of the union when traffic is resumed, your application for re-employment will be favourably considered.

In response to what was an effective banning of the union, a strike was called and, on 26 August, trams around the city came to a standstill and drivers and conductors walked away. That evening Larkin addressed the ITGWU tram workers at Liberty Hall: 'This is not a strike; it is a lockout of the men who have been tyrannically treated by a most unscrupulous scoundrel. We will demonstrate in O'Connell Street. It is our street as well as William Martin Murphy's.'

Larkin had announced that he would speak to a meeting in O'Connell Street on Sunday 28 August. The meeting was promptly banned, but Larkin promised to appear anyway. Disguised in a heavy beard, Larkin spoke from a balcony window in the Imperial Hotel (owned by William Martin Murphy!) before being arrested.

The Dublin Metropolitan Police (DMP) rushed on the workers gathered to listen to Larkin in a vicious baton charge. Men, women and children were felled and beaten as

James Larkin. *Courtesy of the Glasnevin Trust Collection*

they lay in the street. Hundreds were admitted to hospitals. James Nolan, a young union member, was beaten so badly that his skull was smashed in. An eye-witness to the killing of Nolan, Captain Monteith of the Irish Volunteers, reported that a mixed patrol of about thirty-five DMP and Royal Irish Constabulary (RIC) attacked Nolan and clubbed him to the ground, leaving him in a pool of blood.

The inquest into James Nolan's death failed to identify anyone for prosecution. In their verdict the jury expressed an inability to decide who had struck the fatal blow. However, they held that death had been caused by a baton wound and not by a bottle thrown from the vicinity of Liberty Hall, as the police had alleged.

The funeral of James Nolan was held on Wednesday 3 September. The doors and windows of Liberty Hall, the headquarters of the ITGWU were heavily draped in black, and a large placard was placed on the front of the building bearing the inscription, 'In memory of one murdered brother'. Over 30,000 strikers wearing the red hand – the badge of the union – on their coats marched in the mourning procession towards Glasnevin Cemetery. A huge contingent of tramway men marched in uniform alongside many individuals whose bandaged heads and generally battered appearance marked them out as the wounded strikers of the campaign.

Stewards marshalled the mourners and kept order in their ranks. They carried pickaxe handles tipped with black crêpe, for protection against attacks from the police. Their duties were not difficult, as it was a silent crowd that tramped steadily along to the mournful strains of the music supplied by two bands in the procession.

Only one incident occurred to interrupt the sombre tone. As the procession entered Sackville Street, a sudden panic seized the crowd. An uneasy horse had given the impression that the police were breaking up the procession. In fear of another baton charge, the mourners fled wildly in all directions, leaving the hearse alone in the centre of the thoroughfare. When it was discovered that the fear of police aggression was groundless, the crowd filed back into line and the march was resumed until it reached the gates of Glasnevin Cemetery.

The great Dublin Lockout ended in triumph for William Martin Murphy, but though the workers had lost the battle they had won the war. No future employer attempted to destroy a trade union – the right of the workers to organise themselves into unions and choose their leaders was finally established.

ᴖ BRENDAN BEHAN ᴖ

You can tell a lot about a person by who attends their funeral, and the final chapter of Brendan Behan's life was characterised by a variety and richness that few of us could muster.

Behan, poet, playwright and author, was born on 9 February 1923 into a republican family in a time of revolution. His mother was a close friend of Michael Collins and his uncle, Peadar Kearney, wrote 'The Soldier's Song'. At the age of sixteen, as a member of Fianna Éireann, the youth organisation of the Irish Republican Army, Brendan embarked on a mission to blow up the Liverpool docks in 1939. He was arrested and sentenced to three years in a borstal.

Released in December 1941, Brendan returned to Dublin, but was again arrested in April 1942 and charged with shooting at a policeman with intent to kill him at a commemoration ceremony in Glasnevin Cemetery. He was sentenced to fourteen years' penal servitude, which he served at Mountjoy Jail, Arbour Hill and the Curragh. It was while he was imprisoned that he learned to speak Irish from native speakers interned with him and began his writing career, which was to make him famous worldwide.

Released in 1946 under a general amnesty, he began writing plays and books that were to place him on an international stage. Fame never rested easy with Brendan. He had long been a heavy drinker (describing himself, on one occasion, as 'a drinker with a writing problem' and claiming 'I only drink on two occasions – when I'm thirsty and when I'm not'). Alas this vice was to be Brendan's downfall and in

Brendan Behan at work.
© *Getty archive*

March 1964 he collapsed at the Harbour Lights bar. He was transferred to the Meath Hospital in central Dublin, where he died on 20 March, aged forty-one.

On a beautiful sunlit morning of 23 March the coffin of Brendan Behan left Donnybrook church and made its way across to his spiritual home on the northside. In its wake followed those who knew him: politicians, actors, singers and poets, the titled and untitled, the famous and the not so famous, the known and unknown. One bearded man who followed the coffin was heard to mutter over and over again 'Brendan knew me'.

When Brendan's coffin arrived at the gates of Glasnevin Cemetery, as a mark of respect the Dublin binmen held their bin lids aloft. Six pallbearers came forward to carry the coffin down the leafy lanes to the Salkeid family grave (his wife's family). At the graveside his close friend Mattie O'Neill, former Curragh internee and ITGWU official, delivered the oration. He finished by saying: 'A great life has gone out of our lives forever and we hear the echoes of that rich inimitable baritone voice singing "wrap up my green jacket in a brown paper parcel. I'll not need it any more".'

Then, in silence, Peter McNulty of the Fianna stepped forward to the head of the grave and sounded the 'Last Post'. As the mourners slowly slipped away towards the city, they heard the strains of 'The Auld Triangle' as it drifted from the doorway of a local public house – but there was one voice missing.

Brendan Behan's grave.
Courtesy of David Cleary,
Glasnevin Trust Collection.

~: MOUNT JEROME :~

As Benjamin Franklin said, 'In this world nothing can be said to be certain, except death and taxes.' So it makes perfect sense that money can be made from burying the dead. This was certainly the belief of the General Cemetery Company of Dublin established by Robert Shaw of Bushy Park.

Originally the company had wanted to open a cemetery in a section of the Phoenix Park, but the commissioner of His Majesty's Wood Forests and Land Revenues had blocked their application. Not to be deterred, the company decided to purchase the lands of Mount Jerome. On 23 January 1836, John Chambre Brabazon, Earl of Meath, sold the house and lands of Mount Jerome to the newly founded General Cemetery Company which was promptly floated on the stock exchange. Its value was set at £12,000 and shares at £10 each. The largest shareholders were Sir Robert Shaw, Sydney Herbert and R. Gray, who each held twenty shares.

Mount Jerome Cemetery was consecrated by the Protestant Archbishop Whatley on 19 September 1836. Five days later the first burial, for infant twins, took place.

The cemetery, comprising twenty-six acres, was a final resting place for the Protestant community of Dublin until the 1920s, when a strike at Glasnevin Cemetery persuaded the management of Mount Jerome to convert it to a multi-denominational cemetery. Since then it has buried people of all creeds. John Louch, whose Tudor-style gate and lodge can still be seen today, designed the cemetery's layout. At first the company used a pre-existing greenhouse as a mortuary chapel, but in 1845 a competition to design a purpose-built chapel was held and William Atkins beat off eleven other applicants to win with his Gothic-style church design. The building was completed in 1847.

A series of walks or paths divides the now forty-seven-acre cemetery, each with its own distinctive name. You have the Guinness Walk, where that famous brewing family have their plot; the Cypress, Laurel, Yew and Hawthorn Walks – named after the trees which once grew on them; and the Nun's Walk – named after the Sisters of Charity who, under Mary Aikenhead, established a convent next door to the cemetery. Originally the company had wanted to buy the land on which the convent was built and had offered a considerable amount for the plot, but the owner, a Quaker named James Webb, had promised it to the nuns and he kept his word. A school was opened on the site in 1851 and a hospice for the terminally ill was established in 1879.

The Orphan Walk is named after the girls of the Masonic Orphan Schools who are buried along its edge. Many of Dublin's Freemasons also chose Mount Jerome as their final resting place. The more sharp-eyed may notice the square, the compass and the all-seeing eye, some of the many Masonic symbols visible on Mount Jerome's headstones.

To date there are over 250,000 interments in Mount Jerome from all walks of life. Amongst its more famous inhabitants are Sir William Wilde, Joseph Sheridan Le Fanu, John Millington Synge, Jack B. Yeats and Sir William Rowan Hamilton.

By the 1970s revenues had fallen and the condition of the cemetery had begun to deteriorate. In 1984 it was put

Mount Jerome Cemetery in 1903.
Courtesy of the National Library of Ireland

into voluntary liquidation and subsequently purchased by
the family of well-known Dublin undertakers, the Masseys.
Under new management this cemetery in Harold's Cross
has gone from strength to strength and many of its former
beauties can be seen on a stroll through its grounds.

~: NURSE ELIZABETH O'FARRELL :~

Sometimes the end of something is really just the beginning, and never was this truer than when a ragged group of men and women woke up in Moore Street on 29 April 1916.

Elizabeth O'Farrell was born at 33 City Quay on 5 November 1883. Her father Christopher, a dockworker, died when she was still young. At sixteen she joined Inghinidhe na hÉireann (Daughters of Ireland), an organisation that espoused the cause of Irish independence. With her friend Julia Grenan she then joined Cumann na mBan in 1914 and was taught the use of firearms by Countess Markievicz. She was heavily involved in the preparations for the 1916 Rising, being a courier for the Military Council of the Irish Republican Brotherhood and during the Rising itself she was attached to the Irish Citizen Army serving in the GPO, the centre of the Rising, as a dispatch carrier.

Towards the end of Easter Week, Patrick Pearse, having seen a family carrying a white flag shot down through a shattered window, decided that he must surrender. James Connolly agreed that the imminent risk of sacrificing further lives must not be tolerated. The other leaders of the Rising argued, wrangled and pleaded to convince them that the fight could be continued, but bitter reality could not be ignored. Tom Clarke, the frail, grey-haired Fenian, wept openly at the final decision.

The task of conveying this surrender to the enemy was entrusted to the dauntless Elizabeth O'Farrell. With Captain Michael O'Reilly's handkerchief tied to a piece of stick, she bravely walked down the street past the dead. The British military assisted her over the barricade and brought her to Tom Clarke's little shop in Parnell Street. There, General Lowe demanded that within a half an hour she must return with Patrick Pearse to the Moore Street barricade, insisting that the only terms acceptable were unconditional surrender.

At 2.30 p.m. Pearse, in his heavy military overcoat and slouched hat, marched down towards the barricade, Elizabeth O'Farrell by his side. Here, he was received by General Lowe, to whom he handed his sword, pistol and ammunition, along with his tin canteen (which contained two large onions).

On the footpath, outside Byrne's shop at the corner of Moore Street, an old wooden bench was brought out. And it was here that Pearse stooped and signed the document of surrender. Elizabeth O'Farrell then bravely agreed to his request to deliver the documents of surrender to the various Dublin outposts of the rebels. Without speaking, and with a smile, he grasped her hand for the last time.

Nurse Elizabeth O'Farrell.
Courtesy of Kilmainham Gaol Museum

After delivering Pearse's orders to the various rebel outposts, Elizabeth was held at Ship Street Barracks and was then imprisoned with a number of other republican women in Kilmainham Gaol until her release a few months later. General Lowe petitioned that clemency be shown towards her for the 'great assistance' she had given in managing the final hours of the Rising.

Elizabeth was engaged to Eamonn Kelly, owner of a silver mine in Chile, but called off the wedding when she realised that she could never leave Ireland. She qualified as a midwife in the National Maternity Hospital, Holles Street, and later worked as a district nurse. She died in 1957 on Bray promenade after suffering a heart attack and was buried in Glasnevin Cemetery. Each year the Elizabeth O'Farrell Medal is presented to the student who achieves the second highest marks in the midwifery exams.

~: NAZI SPY :~

There is no headstone on the grave NH 286, but if there was it might read: 'John Francis O'Reilly, civil servant, trainee monk, Nazi collaborator, spy and hotel proprietor.'

John Francis O'Reilly was born on 7 August 1916 in Kilkee, County Clare, into a family of seven. His father Bernard 'Casement' O'Reilly was an RIC sergeant and received his dubious nickname because he helped to arrest Roger Casement, a leading member of the Irish Volunteers who had landed at Banna Strand from a German U-boat in 1916.

Young O'Reilly was educated at Kilkee National School and Kilrush Christian Brothers School. He successfully passed the civil service clerical officer's examination in April 1936 and was appointed to the Customs and Excise office at Rosslare, County Wexford.

After eighteen months' service O'Reilly resigned, saying he was 'dissatisfied with the salary and prospects'. In 1939 he decided to join the monks at Buckfast Abbey, but left after a few weeks because he didn't like it.

After a series of jobs, including kitchen porter, door-to-door book salesman and digging air raid shelters, O'Reilly went to Jersey to work as a farm labourer. In June 1940, when Jersey was evacuated, he chose to stay and was recruited as an English-speaking overseer and translator for the German military who employed civilian workers.

In September 1941 he was sent to Berlin to work for the Ministry for Propaganda giving out daily broadcasts

John Francis O'Reilly. *Courtesy of* The Irish Times

under the pseudonym 'Pat O'Brien'. His broadcasts included military and political commentaries on the course of the war from the German standpoint.

Recruited in Berlin by the SS he was parachuted into Ireland on 15 December 1943. He presented himself at Kilkee garda station, where he told the superintendent, without hesitation, that he had 'jumped out of a plane and come down by parachute this morning at Moveen' and, producing his passport, asked if he had broken any law. The superintendent replied that his method of entry into the state was a breach of the Emergency Powers Regulations, according to which arrivals and departures from the state could only be made at designated seaports and airports. O'Reilly then inquired, 'If I had landed by parachute at one of these airports would my entry have been in order?'

He was detained under the Offences Against the State Act, and imprisoned in Arbour Hill, where he remained until 4 July 1944 when he escaped. Following his escape, a nationwide manhunt was mounted; wanted posters were issued offering a £500 reward. Making his way back to his family home in Kilkee, O'Reilly was eventually re-arrested after his father contacted the local police.

On 17 July 1944 his father wrote to the garda superintendent at Kilrush:

> I beg to apply for the reward offered for the arrest of John Francis O'Reilly who escaped from Arbour Hill Barracks on 6th inst. Bernard O'Reilly.

The question of O'Reilly himself ultimately benefiting from the reward for his own recapture was the subject of correspondence between military intelligence and the garda authorities. It was decided that, despite obvious reservations, the reward should be paid, as there had been no restriction put on the source of the information when the garda notice was issued.

Released in 1945, O'Reilly became part owner of the Esplanade Hotel, Parkgate Street, Dublin, and received further notoriety when he was arrested in 1947 and fined £3 for possession of a Webley revolver and fifty rounds of ammunition.

O'Reilly married shortly after his release and fathered six children. The marriage broke up and the children were taken into care. The body of his wife Helen was found in Hume Street on 18 April 1956. She was the victim of a botched abortion performed by the infamous Nurse Cadden, who was convicted and sentenced to death for Helen's death. The sentence was later commuted to penal servitude for life. Helen O'Reilly lies in an unmarked grave, TL 60 in St Patrick's section in Glasnevin.

O'Reilly worked abroad for many years before returning to work in the Shannon industrial estate in the early 1960s. He remarried and fathered another child. At the age of fifty-five he was seriously injured in a road accident in London and died in the Middlesex Hospital on 4 May 1971. His body was brought back to Ireland by his son.

⌁ 'THE FOOLS, THE FOOLS, THE FOOLS' ⌁

Funerals usually signal the end of an era, but sometimes they can herald a new beginning, as in the case of the burial of Jeremiah O'Donovan Rossa.

The old Fenian O'Donovan Rossa died in the USA on 29 June 1915. His widow, a Fenian herself, was determined that he should lie in Irish soil and after a short struggle she obtained permission for his remains to be taken back to the country of his birth. When Tom Clarke, another old Fenian, received the news from America, he realised the potential support that could be aroused in the Irish people for independence, and sent a telegram simply stating: 'Send his body home at once.'

Clarke immediately sprang into action, organising a funeral committee which included some men and women who became household names within a year. Chief marshal for the funeral was Thomas MacDonagh, who worked

Jeremiah O'Donovan Rossa.
Courtesy of the Glasnevin Trust Collection

very closely with Clarke on the plans for the procession to Glasnevin Cemetery. James Connolly and Arthur Griffith sat on the committee alongside Constance Markievicz, Major John MacBride, Cathal Brugha, Edward Daly, Brian O'Higgins and Éamon de Valera.

Poignantly, the committee itself had a tragic destiny: MacDonagh, Connolly, Clarke, MacBride and Daly were all dead within the year, executed in Kilmainham Gaol for their part in the 1916 Rising. In 1922 two more committee members were buried not far from O'Donovan Rossa. Arthur Griffith died from a brain haemorrhage, while Cathal Brugha went down in a hail of bullets behind the Gresham Hotel in the first few days of fighting in the Irish Civil War.

On the day of O'Donovan Rossa's funeral special trains came to Dublin from all over the country. The funeral cortège was a grand affair with pipe bands and armed units of the Irish Volunteers and the Irish Citizen Army following the hearse and the mourning coach. Crowds thronged the streets. At Glasnevin it is reported that some 70,000 people managed to get within earshot of the graveside oration.

After the funeral mass, said by Fr O'Flanagan, there was only one graveside speaker. Patrick Pearse had been Tom Clarke's choice to give the oration. Many on the committee had disputed this, but Clarke knew his man and insisted that he was the one for the job. Pearse spent days and nights in his Connemara cottage writing and re-writing the speech until he felt it was ready. Having shown the speech to no one, Pearse, in the uniform of an Irish Volunteer officer, took the note from his pocket, stood at the end of the grave, and gave what was to become one of the most famous funeral orations in history.

Mourners gathered around the graveside of O'Donovan Rossa during the funeral. *Courtesy of the Glasnevin Trust Collection*

Pearse's finely crafted words not only caught the zeitgeist of the day but were to resonate for generations to come. Even today, when O'Donovan Rossa's name is mentioned, many of us find ourselves muttering Pearse's famous closing line: 'the fools, the fools, the fools! – They have left us our Fenian dead, and while Ireland holds these graves, Ireland unfree shall never be at peace.'

As the old Fenian was laid to rest in the country of his birth, a country he had spent his life fighting for, a new dawn had risen for a generation as they passed out through Glasnevin Cemetery's gates.

~ THE SEAPOINT TRAGEDY ~

We all know Molly Malone died of a fever, but many Dubliners have died over the years from eating her wares, and no story is more tragic than that of a young family from Seapoint, which lies between Blackrock and Monkstown.

On Monday 30 June 1890, Annie, the thirteen-year-old daughter of James O'Connor, a journalist for the *United Ireland* newspaper, was playing in the back garden of No. 1 Seapoint Terrace. Behind the house and adjacent to the railway line was a pond, which had been there for over 100 years. On that day, a handyman, William Mullan, drained some of the water from the pond and, as the water drained, a number of mussel beds became visible. Since the water was salty, William deduced that they had come into the pond during a high tide, as it was believed that the water came from the nearby sea.

Annie O'Connor and the family maid, Eliza Casey, saw the mussel beds and began to gather them. They returned to their kitchen where the mussels were steamed and served with vinegar to the two girls, Annie's mother and her four sisters. Within twenty minutes some of the children said they felt a prickly sensation in their hands. This was followed by vomiting and swelling of the face. Eliza and the youngest child, Moya, had eaten only one or two of the toxic mussels but, nonetheless, became violently ill.

Three doctors arrived on the dreadful scene and gave the children an emetic, but it was too late. Within two short hours, Mrs Mary O'Connor, and four of her children – Annie, Aileen, Kathleen and Norah – were dead.

The coroner's inquest, held two weeks later in Blackrock Town Hall, concluded that the pond had a number of sewage outlets leading into it and that the water had been stagnant for some time, thus causing the mussels to become poisonous. There had been a call for the pond to be condemned ten years previously, but no action had been taken.

The funeral of the O'Connor family was a heartbreaking affair. At 9.30 a.m. the remains of Mrs O'Connor and her four children were enclosed in coffins of oak, the lid of each covered by flowers sent from women in Blackrock. In the leading hearse was placed the coffin of Mrs O'Connor, and in the hearses behind, those of her daughters.

The funeral made its way from Seapoint, through Blackrock to the city centre and then on to Glasnevin Cemetery. The extent of public sympathy was evident – large groups of people gathered and lifted their hats or blessed themselves

O'Connor family grave depicting the wife and children who tragically died. *Author's collection*

as the cortège passed them by. Shops and windows were closed without exception. When the procession reached the cemetery, the remains were brought into the mortuary chapel where last prayers were said before the five coffins were lowered into a single grave beside the O'Connell Circle.

The Seapoint Tragedy, as it became known, shocked the people of Dublin and was spoken about for years. James Joyce, whose father Stanislaus was at the funeral, immortalised it in *Ulysses* when Bloom says: 'Poor man O'Connor's wife and five children poisoned by mussels here. The sewage.'

The grave memorial to his family, erected by the friends of James O'Connor, features a woman and four cherubs who represent the young family: Mary O'Connor, aged thirty-five; Annie O'Connor, aged thirteen; Aileen O'Connor, aged eleven; Kathleen O'Connor, aged seven and Norah O'Connor, aged five.

In later life Moya, the only surviving child, went on to marry Sinn Féin MP Compton Llewelyn Davies, and they settled in London. Moya became a close confidante and courier for Michael Collins. She had been a writer and assisted Collins with his book *The Path to Freedom*. Her translation, with George Thompson, of *Fiche Bliain ag Fás*, Múiris Ó Súilleabháin's autobiography *Twenty Years A-Growing*, describing his youth on the Great Blasket Islands, is probably her best-known work. She also wrote an autobiography, but sadly this memoir was never published, and the manuscript has been lost.

~: IVY DAY :~

Massive celebrity funerals are nothing new. On 10 October 1891 Dublin saw one of the largest funerals ever to take place in the country, when the uncrowned king of Ireland was finally laid to rest in Glasnevin Cemetery.

Charles Stewart Parnell came to prominence in the 1880s during a conflict between tenant farmers and their landlords. He enjoyed an influential political career until his spectacular fall from grace when, in 1890, he was cited in a divorce case involving his long-time lover Kitty O'Shea. The revelation that he was involved with a married woman divided opinion in Ireland and he was deposed as leader of the Irish Parliamentary Party.

Parnell spent his last year trying to garner political support. Despite illness, and a warning from his doctor not to do so, he kept an engagement to speak at Creggs, County Galway, on 27 September 1891. He did so in torrential

Charles Stewart Parnell.
Courtesy of the Glasnevin Trust Collection

Parnell lying in state. *Courtesy of the Glasnevin Trust Collection*

rain, before returning to Dublin and then travelling on to Brighton with what he described as a chill, but which seems to have been more serious than that. He died suddenly in Brighton on 6 October 1891 at the age of forty-five, just five months after he had married Kitty O'Shea.

The pro-Parnell faction of his party quickly stepped in to arrange his funeral. His coffin arrived by boat in Dun Laoghaire at 7.30 a.m. on 10 October where vast crowds had gathered. Members of the DMP had to baton-charge the masses to dissuade them from tearing mementos from the black material covering Parnell's hearse. The coffin was loaded onto a train and arrived in Westland Row within thirty minutes.

There a guard of honour of GAA men carrying hurley

Parnell's funeral car. *Courtesy of the Glasnevin Trust Collection*

sticks wrapped in black cloth greeted the entourage. Thousands of mourners lined Dublin's streets as the coffin made its way towards City Hall, where it was to lie in state. The interior was adorned with black material and thousands of wreaths were placed at the foot of the funeral bier, including one which read, 'My dear, my husband, my king, from his broken-hearted wife'; beside this lay two small bunches of flowers and a card saying 'From Little Clare and Little Kittie to our dear mother's husband'. Parnell's wife Kitty was too distraught to travel and stayed in Brighton. It is an interesting fact that despite having such a visible impact on Irish history, she herself never visited Ireland.

The original plan was for the remains to rest in City Hall until noon for viewing, but the extent of the crowds dictated

Parnell's funeral. *Courtesy of the Glasnevin Trust Collection*

Ivy day in Glasnevin Cemetery 1892.
Courtesy of the Glasnevin Trust Collection

that two extra hours be added. In the few hours that Parnell lay in City Hall, over 40,000 people passed through its doors.

At 2.45 p.m. the procession left City Hall: the hearse drawn by six coal-black horses and surrounded by Parnell's parliamentary colleagues; behind them was led Parnell's favourite horse 'Home Rule', saddled but riderless, followed by a strong body of Clan na Gael led by two old Fenians, James Stephens and John O'Leary; then came a carriage containing Parnell's brother Henry and sister Emily, followed by lord mayors and representatives of corporations from towns across Ireland, and with 60,000 citizens bringing up the rear on foot.

The head of the procession didn't reach Glasnevin Cemetery until three hours later. However, the dense crowds that had gathered made it impossible for the hearse to enter. In the ensuing struggle the police were forced to abandon all attempts to drive the masses back. The funeral was sent into disarray, until eventually, over an hour later, the coffin was brought in through a lower gate. It was placed on a specially constructed platform allowing the crowds to file past.

When, by 8 p.m., there seemed no likelihood that the stream of mourners would end, it was decided to go ahead with the burial. GAA and Clan na Gael men managed to clear a path and form a circle around the grave. The crush was said to be terrible. Crying women, wailing children and the shouts of men struggling within the throng made the Church of Ireland service inaudible and the two reverends were obliged to cut it short.

Parnell's coffin was then lowered into the ground. It was his wish to be buried with 'the common men and women of Ireland' and so the Cemetery Committee had sited his grave on poor ground. Tons of earth had been placed on top of an 1849 cholera grave and Parnell was to be buried in the mound. As the earth was placed over the uncrowned king of Ireland, the hordes of mourners continued to file past. This went on until after midnight. As they left the cemetery, many picked little sprigs of ivy that grew thereabouts and, from that day forward, the anniversary of Parnell's death became known as Ivy Day. Every year a crowd wearing ivy visits Parnell's grave in Glasnevin Cemetery and the Parnell Society organises a speaker to give a short talk on the relevance of Parnell today. This anniversary is the longest continuing event in the cemetery and is now in its uninterrupted 120th year.

~: LUKE KELLY :~

Luke Kelly – socialist, worker, singer and musician – sang with a conviction and honesty that was easy to hear. His like we shall never know again.

Kelly was born in Lattimore Cottages, Sheriff Street, on either 16 November or 16 December 1940. His mother used to say November, but his birth certificate stated December. Luke always took his mother's word for it, because, as he said, 'she was there at the time'.

Luke Kelly. © *Getty images*

The family was a large, close one. Luke's father, another Luke, worked for Jacob's, the biscuit makers. Educated at Laurence O'Tooles in Seville Place, Luke left school at thirteen to ride a messenger boy's bicycle. And in the footsteps of his father, his mother and the rest of the family, he went to work in Jacob's when he was fourteen. He later worked for a time as a docker, a builder, a drain digger and a furniture remover, before leaving for England in 1957 and it was here that his passion for both music and politics came alive.

It is said that Luke was working as a vacuum cleaner salesman in Newcastle when he bought his first banjo. In London he met Dominic Behan, who introduced him to the folk music of northern England and Scotland. Soon, he became a name around the ballad clubs, singing and strumming a banjo. After two and a half years he shouldered his banjo and went to France, where he sang on the streets of Paris.

Luke returned to his native Dublin in 1962 and quickly became a central figure in the city's burgeoning folk music community. O'Donoghue's pub was already established as a session house and soon Luke was singing with, among others, Ronnie Drew and Barney McKenna.

A concert John Molloy organised in the Hibernian Hotel led to his Ballad Tour of Ireland with the Ronnie Drew Ballad Group (billed in one town as the Ronnie Drew Ballet Group!). The success of this led to gigs in the Abbey Tavern and the Royal Marine Hotel, and then to jam-packed sessions in the Embankment, Tallaght. Ciarán Bourke joined the group, followed later by John Sheahan. They renamed themselves 'The Dubliners' at Luke's suggestion, as he was reading James Joyce's book of short stories, entitled *Dubliners*, at the time.

'The Dubliners' went on to win world acclaim and a place in Irish folk-music legend, thanks in no small part to Luke's distinctive, powerful voice. As Ronnie Drew said, 'he sang in perfect diction'.

On 30 June 1980, during a concert in the Cork Opera House, Luke Kelly collapsed on the stage. He had already suffered for some time from headaches and forgetfulness, which had been wrongly ascribed to his alcohol consumption. A brain tumour was diagnosed. Although he toured with the Dubliners after enduring an operation, Kelly's health deteriorated further. He forgot lyrics and had to take

Luke Kelly's grave marker.
Courtesy of David Cleary, Glasnevin Trust Collection.

longer breaks in concerts, as he felt weak. After another operation in 1983 he spent Christmas with his family, but was taken into hospital again in the New Year and died on 30 January 1984.

Hundreds of neighbours from Luke's birthplace mingled with friends from the entertainment world such as Barney McKenna, John Sheahan and Jim McCann at his funeral. John Cannon, Éamonn Campbell, Finbar Furey and Nigel Warren-Green played the songs that had made Luke famous throughout the world. His widow, Deirdre O'Connell, sisters Betty and Mona, brothers John, Jimmy and Paddy, and his friend Madeline Seller wept as the mass opened with the lament 'Róisín Dubh'.

The funeral mass, at an overflowing Whitehall church, ended with many people in tears, as his coffin was wheeled from the church to the strains of 'The Auld Triangle'. Even before the hearse began its short journey to Luke's final resting place in Glasnevin Cemetery, hundreds of people had gathered at the gates to pay their respects to one of their own.

One man at the graveside was so overcome with emotion that he took a handful of clay and clenched it tightly throughout the ceremony in memory of the departed musician. After prayers by Fr Tom Stack, the coffin was lowered by Luke's brothers into his grave, to rest beside those of his father and mother.

The inscription above his grave says simply: 'Luke Kelly, Dubliner 1940–1984'.

⁓ THOMAS STEELE ⁓

At a few minutes before seven o'clock in the morning, on 26 April 1848, Thomas Steele took a last sip of coffee and left Peel's Coffee House, London, for Wellington Bridge. Once there, he placed his hat onto the bridge and then silently threw himself into the Thames, hoping to die. O'Connell had been 'the Liberator' and Steele was known as 'the Pacificator' – they both wore caps with ribbons stating their roles.

Ironically, for a man who had been one of the most eminent water engineers of his day, he had forgotten to check the tides, and sadly, it was out. Thomas Steele plunged into the mire, and merely fumbled around in the mud until a passing Thames waterman pulled him out and brought him to the King's College Hospital. He was discharged after a couple of days, tried for attempting suicide, which was illegal at this time, and given a warning. He returned to Peel's Coffee House where he died within a few weeks, on 15 June.

Thomas Steele was born in Derrymore, County Clare, in 1788, the only child of William Steele and Catherine Bridgeman. The Steeles were a Somerset family, one of whom served with distinction in Monmouth's Regiment during the reign of Charles II. They were rewarded with lands near Nenagh, County Tipperary, from where a branch of the family moved into Clare in the early years of the eighteenth century. His father, William, died during his son's infancy.

Tom showed early signs of intellectual ability. He went on to be educated at Trinity College, Dublin and Magdalene College, Cambridge, from where he graduated with a

Master of Arts degree in 1820. He was described as an elegant classical scholar but, more particularly, he directed his attention to mathematics, mechanics and the application of chemistry to the arts.

Over the next two decades Tom tried his hand at love (the object of his ardour being a less-than-enthusiastic Matilda Crowe), war (against Ferdinand VII of Spain) and invention (of a diving bell), but it was with Daniel O'Connell and the Catholic Association that he found his true calling. Although a Protestant, he was one of the earliest members of the association and became its vice-president. In 1828 he seconded Daniel O'Connell's nomination to run for the parliamentary seat for Clare against Vesey Fitzgerald.

O'Connell named Tom Steele head pacificator follow-ing his efforts in putting down the faction fights and local differences throughout Ireland which so weakened the popular cause. After Catholic emancipation was achieved in

Thomas Steele.
Courtesy of the Glasnevin Trust Collection

1829, Tom Steele remained by O'Connell's side for the next two decades, as he spent his time and family fortune in the cause of repeal of the union.

His presence at O'Connell's monster meetings could not be described as subtle – dressed as an undertaker and carrying a coffin marked 'Repeal', Tom sat on a hearse drawn by six black-plumed horses. When not dressed as an undertaker, he wore a shako (military hat) and military frock. His trousers, often mud-splattered from driving horses, stopped just below his kneecaps. In this odd attire, Tom would sometimes stop on the streets of Ennis and address a speech to his followers, and they would loudly cheer and applaud.

Steele was devoted to O'Connell, saying that he would readily die for him or his country. They travelled around Ireland together addressing crowds and, when there was a threat of violence, Tom Steele would calm the sometimes-fractious mob.

By the 1840s Tom Steele had become something of a figure of fun amongst the new and younger members of the repeal movement. In his adventures he had broken most of his teeth and, when he spoke, he tended to cover the listener in spittle. He was mocked for his slave-like devotion to O'Connell and was described by some of the Young Irelanders as a 'semi-lunatic'. When O'Connell was asked once why he kept Steele on as head pacificator, he responded, 'Why, who else would want that job?'

In 1843 a split occurred between Daniel O'Connell and the Young Irelanders. Steele took the side of his chief and watched as the repeal movement, and their decades of work, fell asunder.

By 1847, with his great friend dead and Ireland devastated by fever and famine, Tom Steele sank into a depression from which he was never to emerge.

After his death his remains were brought to Ireland, waked in Conciliation Hall, Dublin, and buried at the foot of Daniel O'Connell's tower in Glasnevin.

Parnell's Grave and O'Connell's tower, Glasnevin 1895.
Courtesy of the Glasnevin Trust Collection

~: HEIL HITLER IN DUBLIN :~

On 23 May 1947, as the war trials were being held across Europe, a funeral car arrived at Deansgrange Cemetery, Dublin, draped with a swastika flag for the burial of Major Hermann Görtz.

Görtz was something of a self-made spy. He had been convicted of espionage in 1936 after copies of plans of Manston Airfield were discovered in his belongings in a house he was renting in Broadstairs, England. Jailed for four years, he was deported to Germany upon his release on parole in February 1939.

In the summer of 1940, Görtz parachuted into Ballivor, County Meath. Rather unwisely for a spy, he was wearing a Luftwaffe uniform and First World War medals when he landed. His mission was to make contact with the IRA and check the feasibility of Plan Kathleen (a plan for a German invasion of Northern Ireland with help from the IRA). However, he soon realised that neither the plan nor the IRA were up to the job. He went into hiding, staying with sympathisers in Wicklow and South County Dublin for about eighteen months.

In November 1941, an IRA member, Pearse Paul Kelly, who was being followed by the police, visited Görtz's hiding place in Dublin. Police swooped in and arrested both.

Görtz was interned until the end of the war. He was first detained in Mountjoy Jail but was later moved to Athlone Military Barracks with nine others. While in captivity, the German spy became slightly unhinged. In Athlone he

The marker for the German military cemetery at Glencree,
County Wicklow. *Author's collection*

practised suicide techniques with a fellow prisoner, carved
an elaborate tombstone for his own grave and, according to
his diary, envisaged taking over the leadership of the IRA.

When he was paroled in 1947, he went to live with
friends in Dublin but was informed he would be deported
to Germany. In May 1947 Görtz reported to the Aliens
Registration Office in Dublin Castle. Terrified that he would
then be turned over to the Soviets, he swallowed a cyanide
capsule. He died at Mercer's Hospital a few hours later.

More than 200 people attended Görtz's funeral. As the
coffin came into the cemetery, the flag was blown off by the
wind, and a woman wearing a swastika badge ran forward

and replaced it. Swastika badges were worn by many of the crowd, mostly made up of women who wept bitterly. A young boy carried a miniature Nazi flag beside two women who wore the ribbons of a 1916 medal. As the coffin was lowered, a young woman stepped up to the graveside and gave a Nazi salute. A young man joined her, gave the salute and whispered 'Heil Hitler'. Wreaths were then placed along the grave. Most were red flowers with black ribbon and cards with lamentations for a true German soldier. While most were anonymous, others had cards attached announcing that they were from Mary, Maise, Bridie or Muriel. Who these women were is unknown.

When the woman who had replaced the flag was asked who she was, she refused to give her name. In fact the only person to give his name was Hans Waider, who told the *Irish Times* journalist, 'I would like my name mentioned. I helped to carry the coffin. I was the only German to do so as I think the rest were Irishmen.'

In 1974 the remains of Hermann Görtz were transferred to the German Military Cemetery at Glencree, County Wicklow.

~: CHOLERA GRAVES :~

The next time you drink a glass of water from a tap in Dublin, be thankful that you're not your nineteenth-century counterpart because, if you were, there's a fair chance you'd be wriggling around on the ground in agony within the hour.

In the year 1832, a disease called 'Asiatic cholera' arrived in Ireland for the first time. It made a couple more visits over the next twenty years, each time claiming thousands of lives. The 1832 cholera was first seen in India in August 1817, spreading throughout the subcontinent. It reached Moscow in 1830 and from there swept westward through France, Belgium, Holland, England, Scotland and then Ireland.

A nineteenth-century satirical cartoon about cholera and its prevention.
Courtesy of the Glasnevin Trust Collection

Cholera is a tiny micro-organism that usually enters the body through the mouth. It kills rapidly through dehydration, usually within three or four days, but sometimes within a few hours. The most common source of infection is water contaminated by the excreta of another cholera sufferer. The dire sanitation conditions in the Dublin slums and tenement houses proved a fertile ground for its proliferation.

The first reported cases of the disease were in the Summerhill area of the city in the first week of July 1832. Of the five people who contracted it, four were dead within thirty hours. The first to die was a labourer, followed quickly by the woman who had washed his dead body. The disease quickly spread across the city to the Liberties, ravaging the population as it went. Within a week there were 500 cases, with 143 deaths in the Liberties alone. By the end of July 3,665 cases had been recorded.

The authorities' response to this devastating epidemic was incompetent at best. The Archbishop of Dublin, Daniel Murray, sent out a pastoral letter to his Dublin flock telling them that this was God's judgement against them. The response of the medicos wasn't much better. With little knowledge of micro-organisms, it was believed that cholera travelled in a fog, which they called a 'miasma', and so recommendations included ventilation of hospitals and homes and the burning of tar and camphor to clear the air. In some cases, the local militia were sent out to fire volley upon volley of shots into the air, in the hope that this would 'purify the heavy atmosphere'. A newspaper article at that time records one such incident in Newry as having 'no immediate result'.

Other remedies included blood-letting, purging, emetics, stimulants, injection of warm water into the veins, and calomel mixed with opium or laudanum, none of which worked. Cholera victims were dehydrating. A simple infusion of water and saline would have stopped this and ultimately saved their lives.

The Central Board of Health for Ireland set up an *ad hoc* committee of two doctors and two laymen. All four were to be paid one guinea a day for their services (the average labourer earned some two guineas per year). They turned the former Richmond Penitentiary at Grangegorman into the city's main cholera hospital, with the adjoining garden used by the lunatics of the Richmond asylum to be set aside as a graveyard for the victims. Because relatives were not permitted to be present at funerals, families were reluctant to allow their sick to enter the hospital, preferring to bury their loved ones in local graveyards, rather than the anonymity of a cholera pit. To avoid detection by Officers of Health, most victims were buried under cover of darkness in parochial graveyards, the most notable being St Paul's and St Michan's. Sometimes victims were buried less ceremoniously, such as the coal porter who died in Templeogue whose corpse was discovered when his knees were seen protruding through a shallow grave in a field.

As the number of deaths mounted, it became difficult to find burial places. Bully's Acre, an ancient public cemetery, refused to allow further burials after 500 bodies were received in a period of ten days.

The cholera epidemic ended in autumn 1833. Over 20,000 cases had been recorded in Dublin. Fifty per cent of the people who contracted cholera died.

Son of a small farmer, Michael Collins was born on 16 October 1890, at Woodfield, Clonakilty, County Cork. He joined the Irish Republican Brotherhood (IRB) while he was working in London and returned to Dublin to fight in the GPO during the 1916 Rising. He was imprisoned until December 1916 and, on his release, became prominent in Sinn Féin and the Volunteer movement, as well as being a member of the Supreme Council of the IRB, a position of considerable influence. In the 1918 British general election, Collins was elected for Cork south and for Tyrone. However, the elected Irish candidates followed an abstentionist policy, refusing to recognise the British Parliament and in January 1919 convened their own parliament, Dáil Éireann. Collins was appointed Minister for Home Affairs and in April 1919 became Minister for Finance.

During the War of Independence, he organised the supply of weapons for the Irish Volunteers and developed a very successful intelligence system. During this period Collins and his close friend Harry Boland vied for the affections of Kitty Kiernan, but it was Collins who won her heart. From the latter half of 1921 until his death, Collins and Kiernan exchanged more than 300 love letters.

A Truce was finally agreed on 11 July 1921, and Collins was chosen as one of the

Kitty Kiernan.
Courtesy of the Glasnevin Trust Collection

Michael Collins. *Courtesy of Mercier Archives*

Irish delegates to negotiate an Anglo-Irish Treaty. Following lengthy debates, the Treaty was signed on 6 December 1921. Collins considered the Treaty as a means towards obtaining a thirty-two county republic and signed it with 'great reluctance'. He subsequently fell into a mood of deep depression and wrote to a close friend: 'I tell you this – early this morning I signed my own death warrant.'

A vicious Civil War (1922–23) followed between the pro-Treaty Free State forces and the anti-Treaty IRA. Collins was commander-in-chief of the pro-Treaty army. On 12 August 1922 Collins' ally and friend Arthur Griffith died of a massive cerebral haemorrhage. He had never recovered from the strain of the Treaty negotiations.

Eight days later, though ill with the stomach trouble that

Collins lying-in-state in Dublin City Hall.
Courtesy of the Glasnevin Trust Collection

Flowers on the grave of Michael Collins 1922.
Courtesy of the Glasnevin Trust Collection

General Eoin O'Duffy laying a wreath on Michael Collins' grave.
Courtesy of the Glasnevin Trust Collection

had plagued him for several months, and suffering from a bad cold, Michael Collins left on a mission to visit troops in his home county of Cork and to uncover IRA funds hidden in the city's banks. Warned not to go, he told his companion, 'They wouldn't shoot me in my own county.' Depressed and ill he set out, some say, to try to end the fighting. At any rate, he visited several anti-Treaty men, although there is no record of what they discussed, as well as inspecting various barracks. On the last day of his life, 22 August 1922, he set out from Cork city in a convoy that passed through Bandon, Clonakilty and Rosscarbery, on its way to Skibbereen.

He stopped at Woodfield and there in the Four Alls, the pub situated across the road from the house where his mother was born, he stood his family and escort a round of the local brew – 'Clonakilty wrastler'.

On the return trip they again passed through Bandon. Michael Collins had only twenty minutes more to live. Around eight o'clock, his convoy was ambushed at a place known as Béal na mBláth, the mouth of flowers. Only one man was killed in the skirmish between his convoy and the IRA ambushers who awaited it – Michael Collins. He was only thirty-one years old.

His funeral was held on 28 August, with the *Irish Independent* reporting on 'the greatest pageant of sorrow ever seen in Dublin: a cortège three miles long'. An estimated 300,000 people lined the streets of the capital, as the funeral procession wound its way to Glasnevin Cemetery. General Richard Mulcahy, the new commander-in-chief of the Free State army, gave the oration at his graveside, referring to Collins as 'the fallen leader, a great hero and a great legend'.

Sexton's Number	Registrar's Number	Latitude	Longitude	NAMES	Adts. Years	Children Years	Months	RESIDENCES
12277	12529	Rg	9	Anne Doyle	35			Glasnevin
78	30	Qg	9	Elizabeth Dunn		10		Burges Lane
83	1	Rg	9	Alicia Brennan		2		Barrack St
				29				
80	2	Rg	9	Bridget Reilly	23			Carter's Lane
86	3	Sg	9	John O'Neill	50			Church St
81	4			Mary Rourke	45			Sandy Mount
	5			Not made use of				
82	6	Rg	9	Catherine Daly	52			Barrack St
84	7	Qg	9	Thomas Stewart		1	3	Golden Lane
88	8			Mary Cahill		3		Patrick Street
85	9	Sg	23	Maria Stewart	22			Penders court
				30				
87	10	Qg	9	John Bolton		9		Essex St
90	1	Sg	9	Alicia Carty	37			New St
89	2			Mary Downey	80			Cumberland St
94	3	Ug	9	Sara Byrne	16			Thomas Court
90	4	Sg	9	Bernard Collins		3		Earl Street
91	5			Mary Leahy	51			Gt Britain St
				31				
301	6	Ug	9	John Coleman	50			Ormond Market
6	7	Qg	9	Thomas Power		1	6	Bride St
96	8	Ug	9	Bridget Knee	60			Gloster Place
293	9	Qg	9	Margaret Quinn		2		Constitution Hill
	30	Eg	9	Patrick Byrne				Phibsborough
92	1	Ug	24	Patrick O'Hearn				Church St
97	2	Sg	31	Andrew McCormick		6		King St
95	3	Qg	9	Margaret Moore		11		Nangle Court
11	4	Vg	9	Catherine Hart	86			Kings Court
302	5	Ug	9	Margaret Wheeler	21			
3	6			Thomas Casy	28			
4	7			Bridget Heyffin	26			} Hardwick Hospl
5	8			William Kelly	16			
99	9	Qg	9	Susan Murray				

The poor ground register for Glasnevin.
Courtesy of the Glasnevin Trust Collection

ᚱ UNMARKED GRAVES ᚱ

There is nothing sadder than an unmarked grave. Yet the cemeteries of Dublin are littered with thousands of these, which have no headstones and lie like silent monuments to human poverty.

In Glasnevin Cemetery alone, a staggering 800,000 people are buried in either 'poor ground' or in unpurchased graves – the final resting places for those who, at the end of their days through whatever circumstances, did not have the price of a grave. One of the guiding principles of the cemetery when Daniel O'Connell opened it in 1832 was to afford the poor of Dublin a place of burial. Their funerals came from the industrial schools, from the Magdalene laundries and the workhouses, or simply the poor tenements of Dublin for people with just pennies in their pockets at the end of their lives.

Amongst the tenements of Dublin, life was one of the cheapest commodities. Tenement houses were structurally feeble death traps. The soft bituminous coal that was burned at that time caused acid rain, which weakened the timbers, slates and brickwork of these formerly grand Georgian buildings, and many collapsed. It was said that even trying to put a nail in a wall to hang a picture could cause the wall to fall to the ground. The risk of fire was so great, with all cooking, cleaning and heating done in the same room on an open fire of turf or coal, that burning tenements were an everyday occurrence.

But disease claimed most lives in the tenements, with

their dire sanitary conditions and gross overcrowding. Tuberculosis, diphtheria, smallpox, typhoid and respiratory problems claimed thousands. Even the layers of damp wallpaper that had built up over the decades were a breeding ground for infection. Shoeless infants walked on roads of dirt and mire, and gangrene took hold in their cut and dirty feet. With the absence of drugs like penicillin, and a diet of bread and tea, their weakened frames could provide little resistance and a simple cut often proved fatal.

A read through the record books of the poor ground for Glasnevin Cemetery tells a tale of poverty and injustice, which was unparalleled in any other part of Europe at that time. The records document the person's name, age, address and occupation. But it is the 'cause of death' that brings a sobering tear to the eye of the reader. Dublin's poor died of 'tooth abscess' (without penicillin infections entered the blood stream and poisoned the body), of 'diarrhoea' (from dehydration), of 'whooping cough', 'scarlatina' and of 'flu', as well as countless other diseases and maladies which a quick visit to the doctor or chemist would cure today.

Of course the most vulnerable in any society are its oldest and youngest, a fact reflected in the death rates of that time. The old would die of 'decline' or 'dropsy' or sometimes 'for want of food'. With a fifty per cent mortality rate, children died in their droves, from everything from 'teething' to 'colic'. Many died from everyday diseases that parents today watch children go through, like mumps and chickenpox. Sometimes you come across the heartbreaking 'died for want of a good midwife', as home births were the norm in the tenements of Dublin.

The poor ground register. *Courtesy of the Glasnevin Trust Collection*

No. 66 Church Street, a tenement house, collapsed on 2 September 1913, killing seven people. A public outcry demanded a new Housing Bill, but it took over fifty years to rid Dublin of its dreadful tenements.

The seven who died in the Church Street disaster are resting in unmarked graves in Glasnevin Cemetery. Their names are Margaret O'Rourke (age fifty-three), Eugene Salmon (age seventeen), Elizabeth Salmon (age eight), Peter Cowley (age six), Eliza Fagan (age forty-three), Nicholas Fitzpatrick (age fifty) and John Sheils (age three).

～ FORGOTTEN SOLDIERS ～

General Douglas MacArthur said, 'old soldiers never die; they just fade away'. But sometimes it is our memory of them that fades, as in the case of Edward Bolger.

Edward Bolger was born in Clontarf, County Dublin, in 1871. The son of a carriage builder, he was unable to find work in his native city and, on his seventeenth birthday, he left Ireland for Liverpool. Initially he worked as a labourer toiling for fifty-five hours a week for a wage of £1. But it wasn't long before he enlisted in the South Lancashire Regiment of the British army on 11 July 1899.

Edwards' first posting was to South Africa for service during the second Anglo-Boer War, where he saw action at the Battle of Spion Kop, and his regiment also took part in the relief of Ladysmith.

When the second Anglo-Boer War ended in 1902, Edward was posted to India for four years. With the start of the First World War, he was sent to France where he landed on 27 August 1914. He served with the 2nd Battalion South Lancashire Regiment until he was badly wounded in the head at Hooge, east of Ypres, on 25 September 1915. The battalion war diary of an officer describes the action in which he was wounded:

> After a bombardment of 30 minutes, the infantry advanced on the enemy trenches but the attack was halted by uncut barbed wire and broken ground. Four men got through to the enemy parapet.
> Casualties for 25 September KIA 26, Wounded 175, Missing 45.

During the battle, a shell had exploded in front of Edward, wounding him terribly, and he lost his left ear, his left eye and also the mobility in part of his left hand. During the battle he had tried to bandage his eye and ear, but the bandage kept falling off as he crawled along the ground. Eventually Edward was found by the army medics and brought to a hospital behind the lines. Here he was given a glass eye and medical care before being discharged due to the severity of his wounds on 27 May 1916. He returned to Dublin and lived at 7 First Avenue, Seville Place. He received four medals for his service: the Queen's South Africa Medal, 1914 Star, British War Medal and Victory Medal. Unable to gain employment, Edward survived on his army pension of nine shillings a week.

On Christmas Day 1916, Edward drowned in the River Liffey. A report in the *Irish Independent* on 27 December records the events which led to his death:

> The body of Edward Bolger, 50 years, ex-soldier was found floating in the Alexandra Basin on Sunday. It is believed that the unfortunate man while crossing from one boat to another fell down between them into the water and was drowned.

With no family coming forward to claim the body, Edward's remains were brought to the North Dublin Union workhouse. On 29 December his body was brought to Glasnevin Cemetery and buried in poor ground. Unmarked for over ninety years, Edward Bolger is buried in grave BJ 333 St Bridget's.

⁓ GRAVEYARD SUICIDE ⁓

On Monday 20 November 1871 a small group of people were gathered in Mount Jerome Cemetery at the funeral of a friend, when their prayers were interrupted by the sudden sound of gunfire coming from the northern part of the cemetery. When two of the men bravely went to investigate, they found Mr John Clibborn lying dead between two headstones with a still smoking pistol clenched in both his hands.

The pistol, an old-fashioned duelling model, appeared to have been overloaded with shot and fired into the mouth of the dead man. The left side of the man's face had been blown away. The part that remained was blackened and burned.

On inspection, the men observed that the dead man was fashionably dressed and of some means. His hat and cane had been placed on an adjacent grave. When they lifted the hat, three pieces of paper fluttered to the ground.

The first was a letter addressed to the managing directors of the Royal Bank, where the dead man had been employed as a manager for the previous twenty-five years. The letter explained that, when the American Civil War had ended, Mr Clibborn had begun to invest in the Wicklow Copper Mines, buying shares at a price of twenty-two pounds each. Initially he had made some money but, as time went on, the price of the shares fell and a friend had lent him money to purchase more. The friend had promised that he would hold the shares as security and would not sell them. Now three years later the friend was in the process of selling the shares

MELANCHOLY SUICIDE OF MR JOHN CLIBBORN.

Mr John Clibborn, manager of the Arran Quay branch of the Royal Bank, committed suicide yesterday morning under circumstances of such a peculiar nature as render the act one of the most distressing it has been our painful duty to record for many years. It appears that at about eleven o'clock a number of persons who were in Mount Jerome Cemetery attending the funeral of a friend, were startled by the report of a pistol which disturbed the solemnity of the mournful ceremony in which they were engaged. As the shot appeared to have been fired at the northern side of the grave yard, some gentlemen at once hastened to the spot and were horrified at finding Mr Clibborn lying between two graves quite dead, with a still smoking pistol firmly clenched in both hands. One of the graves contained the body of his child. The pistol was one of the old fashioned duelling weapons, and from the shocking appearance of the body it is evident that the pistol was heavily charged and that the dreadful act was committed with great determination. The nature of the wound would lead to the, belief that the deceased gentleman must have placed the muzzle of the pistol in his mouth when firing, for the left side of his face was completely blown away, as well as a portion of the roof of the skull, the part of the face remaining was blackened and discoloured. The deceased, who was a young man, was fashionably dressed, and inside his hat, which lay on the ground beside him was pinned a sheet of foolscap paper on which was written a statement that up to the present time gives the only cause assignable for the dreadful act. It is stated that at an earlier period of the morning Mr Clibborn arrived at his office in his usual health, and having transacted some business told the cashier that he was going out for a short time, and that if he did not return in a couple of hours they need not expect him before the time appointed had expired. A gentleman arrived at the bank with the sad intelligence that he had just seen Mr Clibborn lying beside the grave of his child in Mount Jerome Cemetery, with his brains blown out. The deceased gentleman was much respected in Dublin. The following was the contents of the document found in his hat :—

Part of a report on the graveyard suicide. *Courtesy of* The Irish Times

115

Mount Jerome Cemetery. *Courtesy of Kilmainham Gaol Museum*

for nine pounds and he, the writer, was ruined. He went on to say that the Wicklow mine had now gone down a hundred fathoms, had hit a rich vein of ore, and would shortly be making money once more. He begged the bank's forgiveness and asked them to grant a small annuity to his wife.

The second letter was addressed to his wife and son, and simply said:

> My Dear Good Wife and Son,
> Forget me. I cannot help myself. I put all I had and more into Wicklow Copper, which all have been sold at nine pounds after costing me twenty-two.
> Your unfortunate, though well meaning,
> John.

The third was a receipt for the purchase of the grave on which he now lay.

Two days later an inquest was held at the County Coroner's Court. Three fellow employees of the bank came forward to say that John Clibborn had been very excited when they had spoken to him in the days before his death. One stated that his hair, usually tight and well groomed, was wild and unkempt. A director for the bank stated that his work had been without blemish.

Finally, Henry Barton came forward and declared that, although he was the friend mentioned in Mr Clibborn's letter, much of what had been written was untrue. Mr Barton explained that he had lent the money without interest and, after three years, had decided to sell the shares to get some of his money back. He said that he had made a gift of £1,600 and agreed with Mr Clibborn that he could pay the remaining £2,000 in small instalments. Mr Barton reported that, in trying to explain his rationale to the usually shrewd and business-like Mr Clibborn, the latter began ranting in an unreasonable and irrational manner.

The verdict was that the deceased, John Clibborn, committed suicide while in a state of temporary insanity. He was buried in Mount Jerome Cemetery on Friday 24 November 1871, in the grave where he took his own life.

Mrs Clibborn was granted an annuity of £5 per annum from the Royal Bank. The Wicklow Copper Mines struck a rich vein of copper ore shortly afterwards ... its shares rocketed in value to £40.

∻ THOMAS ASHE ∻

Born in 1885, in the small village of Lispole, near Dingle, County Kerry, Thomas Ashe was educated locally. He qualified as a teacher in the De La Salle Teacher Training College in Waterford city, later taking up the position of principal at Corduff National School in Lusk, County Dublin.

Ashe played an important role in the nationalist movement and was a member of the Irish Volunteers and Conradh na Gaeilge. Through his links with these organisations, he was recruited into the Irish Republican Brotherhood and was chosen to visit America on a fundraising trip. During his time there he met the likes of John Devoy, Joe McGarrity and Roger Casement.

The years leading up to the 1916 Rising saw Ashe take on more prominent roles in the republican movement, and by Easter Sunday 1916 he was the commanding officer of the Dublin 5th Battalion (Fingal) of the Volunteers. During the Rising, Ashe and his battalion of just forty-eight men led many successful attacks and ambushes on military barracks around the north Dublin area. They

Thomas Ashe.
Courtesy of Mercier Archives

successfully demolished the Great Northern Railway Bridge, disrupting access to the capital. In addition, they captured the Royal Irish Constabulary (RIC) barracks at Ashbourne, County Meath, in a fight that lasted six hours, during which time eleven RIC men were killed and over twenty were wounded. By comparison, the Fingal Battalion lost only two men and five were wounded. Ashe and his men also captured three other police barracks along with large quantities of arms and ammunition, which enabled them to keep their guerrilla war going.

When news of the surrender reached Thomas Ashe he laid down his arms and was arrested, court-martialled and sentenced to death. The sentence was later commuted to life imprisonment. He was released as part of the general amnesty in June 1917 and immediately became involved once more in the independence movement. He was elected president of the Irish Republican Brotherhood, taking the place of the executed Patrick Pearse.

Ashe travelled the country campaigning for Sinn Féin, with the British authorities deeming his speeches to be 'calculated to cause disaffection'. He was re-arrested for sedition and incitement of the population on 15 July 1917 and was sent to Mountjoy Jail. He demanded that he be given prisoner of war status, including the right to wear his own clothes and associate with his fellow inmates. When the authorities refused their demands, Ashe and six of his fellow inmates went on hunger strike.

All requests to Ashe to end the hunger strike were refused. He was adamant in his conviction stating: 'They have branded me a criminal. Even though if I die [sic], I die

Thomas Ashe's funeral leaving City Hall, Dublin.
Courtesy of the Glasnevin Trust Collection

Gun salute at Thomas Ashe's funeral. *Courtesy of Mercier Archives*

in a good cause'. Ashe and his fellow prisoners were put in straitjackets and force-fed. Administered by a trainee doctor, the process was brutal. On the third day, Ashe collapsed shortly after the procedure. It was later discovered that, among other complications, the feeding tube had pierced his lung. He was immediately taken to the nearby Mater Hospital. Two days later Ashe died of heart and lung failure.

After lying in state at City Hall, Ashe's cortège made its way through Dublin to Glasnevin Cemetery on 30 September 1917. It is estimated that 30,000 people lined the streets, some having travelled great distances to attend.

At the graveside, three Volunteers fired a volley and then Michael Collins stepped forward to make a short but poignant speech, in English and *as Gaeilge*, leaving the Irish population in no doubt as to what was needed to gain independence. His English words were:

> Nothing additional remains to be said. That volley which we have just heard is the only speech which it is proper to make above the grave of a dead Fenian.

The death of Thomas Ashe had a resounding effect on the attitude of the Irish people. The Rising of 1916 now became the focal point of passion because of the sacrifices of the signatories of the Proclamation. The brutal manner of Ashe's death, coupled with the summary executions of the 1916 leaders, galvanised the nation. Committees sprang up all over the country to pay tribute to the memory of this brave man, and indirectly fuelled the fire that led to Irish independence.

36th (Ulster) Division parade outside Belfast City Hall, 1915.
Courtesy of Kilmainham Gaol Museum

UVF in Belfast, 1913. *Courtesy of Kilmainham Gaol Museum*

~: STRANGE BEDFELLOWS :~

They say politics makes strange bedfellows but, to my mind, graveyards make the strangest bedfellows of them all. Such is the case of Richard Simpson, a Belfast loyalist who signed the Ulster Covenant and ended up being buried side by side with Irish Volunteers and members of the Irish Citizen Army in the Republican Plot in Glasnevin Cemetery.

Richard Simpson was born in Belfast in 1877. Presbyterian in faith, he married Ann Jane Briggs in St Anne's Church in 1900 and lived in Downing Street, Belfast, just off the Shankill Road. He and his wife adopted his three nieces, Effra, Ann Jane and Robina, when his sister, their mother, died. Richard earned his living as a casual labourer.

In 1912, as a protest against the Third Home Rule Bill, Sir Edward Carson drafted the Ulster Covenant, which asked people to defeat the present conspiracy to set up a 'Home Rule Parliament in Ireland'. On 28 September 1912, 471,414 men and women across Ireland followed Edward Carson, the first signatory, and declared their resistance to any form of Irish independence. Richard Simpson was one of these. One year later, when the Ulster Volunteer Force (UVF) was founded, Richard, as a signatory of the covenant, became a member.

When the First World War broke out, 90,000 members of the UVF joined the British army and made up the 36th (Ulster) Division. Richard Simpson followed them into the army when he enlisted into the Royal Irish Regiment in Belfast on 12 April 1915. A month later, due to his being unfit

Carson signing the Ulster Covenant. *Courtesy of Kilmainham Gaol Museum*

for overseas service, Rifleman Simpson was sent to the 18th Battalion (reserve) of the regiment. As his comrades from the UVF were fighting in France, Richard was transferred to the Royal Irish Fusiliers in Wellington Barracks, Dublin (now Griffith College) on 31 March 1916.

Two days before the 1916 Rising started, on 22 April 1916, three soldiers entered a room in Wellington Barracks. They later testified that, on entering, they could smell a strong smell of gas. In the room they found the motionless body of Richard Simpson. A coroner's inquest was ordered and the body was placed in the barracks' morgue, but the coroner's inquest never took place. As the city burned with the flames of insurrection, the body of the rifleman from Belfast was simply forgotten about.

During the Easter rebellion, General Maxwell had declared martial law and no funerals took place. The bodies of those killed during the Rising were wrapped in canvas and held in Dublin Castle. Some were temporarily buried but most were laid out in the Upper Square. On 1 May, with the rebellion over, the first funerals were allowed, and over 250 corpses were transported across a shell-shocked city to Glasnevin Cemetery. Amongst these were the remains of Rifleman Simpson.

In Glasnevin, a trench had been dug in the St Paul's section of the cemetery. It was eight graves wide and thirty graves long. Into this trench were placed the remains of the Irish Volunteers and Irish Citizen Army, who had fallen in battle for the Republic and with them, wearing the uniform of a British soldier, are the mortal remains of a proud member of the UVF.

∵ CIVIL WAR GRAVES ∵

The great bard Christy Moore sings that 'everyone in the graveyard votes the same'. But while they lived, their politics often drove them to desperate acts, dividing countries, communities and even families. Nowhere is this more apparent than during the Irish Civil War.

On 8 December 1922, along with three other anti-Treaty republicans (Liam Mellows, Richard Barrett and Joe McKelvey), Rory O'Connor was executed by firing squad in reprisal for the anti-Treaty IRA's killing of a Free State TD, Seán Hales. Although each man was incarcerated in Mountjoy Jail at the time of Hales' killing, they were selected for execution by the state on the basis that they were prominent leaders of the anti-Treaty forces. Each man came from a different province and so their selection also served as a national warning of the measures the Provisional Government were prepared to take.

Rory O'Connor's execution order was given by the then Justice Minister Kevin O'Higgins who, less than a year earlier, had asked him to be best man at his wedding.

An eyewitness account from Hugo McNeill, officer in charge of the firing squad, recalls:

> At 8 a.m. the officer in charge of the firing squad gave the order to fire. The majority of those in the firing squad aimed at Rory O'Connor. We had detailed five members to fire at each prisoner but this didn't happen. Rory O'Connor fell dead immediately. There were so many bullets in him that his clothes went on fire.
>
> None of the other prisoners were dead after the first

volley. Two of them were on the ground. I walked over and gave them the *coup de grâce* by revolver.

While I was doing this, Joe McKelvey cried to the Medical Officer: 'For Christ's sake, kill me, Doc!'

The doctor, seeing that I was standing in a daze, pulled me away from the other men and grabbed me by my Sam Browne belt and pulled me down until I was close to Joe McKelvey, who said: 'Another one!' I then shot him in the chest through the paper target. But it wasn't enough and he repeated: 'Another one!' This I gave him, and I was satisfied he was dead.

The Irish Civil War dragged on for almost another year, decimating a fledgling state and dividing families and friends for decades to come.

Rory O'Connor was buried in Mountjoy Jail graveyard until 8 November 1924, when, together with eight others, his body was brought to Glasnevin Cemetery for interment in the Republican Plot. Although rain fell heavily, large crowds assembled on the pavements of Dublin, to witness this poignant spectacle.[3]

In retaliation for Kevin O'Higgins' role in the executions, the anti-Treaty IRA killed his father and burned his family home in Stradbally, County Laois. Anti-Treaty members later shot O'Higgins himself, as he left mass in Booterstown, County Dublin, in 1927. His funeral took place on 13 July after a requiem mass at St Andrew's church, Westland Row. The funeral cortège stretched for three miles along crowded streets. O'Higgins was buried in St Brigid's section, Glasnevin Cemetery, in the same grave as his infant son.

---

3   Liam Mellows is buried in Castletown, County Wexford; Joe McKelvey is buried in Milltown Cemetery in Belfast; Barrett is now buried in his home county of Cork, in Ahiohill churchyard.

Kevin O'Higgins' funeral. *Courtesy of the National Library of Ireland*

Former friends, latter enemies, Rory O'Connor and Kevin O'Higgins both lie in silent graves within the walls of Glasnevin Cemetery.

~: BULLY'S ACRE :~

Bully's Acre sounds like the type of place you might lose your pocket money, but it happens to be one of Dublin's oldest burial grounds. The name Bully is simply a corruption of the word 'bailey' or 'bailiff'. A bailey is the furthermost field from a castle while a bailiff acts on behalf of a landlord, so Bully's Acre was either an acre in the possession of the landlord's agent or an acre on the outskirts of a castle's lands.

Encompassing just three and half acres, the cemetery was in use from the time of St Maigneann, who founded a church there in AD 606, giving the locality its name Kilmainham (Cill Maigneann). It was the choice of burial place for many a Celtic warrior. It has been cited as the place where Brian Boru's son Murrough and his grandson Turlough were buried after the Battle of Clontarf. Robert Emmet was buried here (albeit briefly – but that's a story for another day) after his execution in nearby Thomas Street.

Ireland's first world champion boxer, Dan Donnelly, found his final resting place here too. Well most of him did anyway! Donnelly was born in Bull Alley in March 1788, the ninth of his mother's seventeen children. He fought at a time when boxing was of the bare knuckles variety and bouts had no time limits. He took part in only three major fights, winning each of them. His second victory against George Cooper in the Curragh, on 13 December 1815, was his most celebrated. Donnelly broke Cooper's jaw in the eleventh round of the twenty-two minute fight, and collected the prize of £60.

Bully's Acre. *Author's Collection*

Dan returned to Dublin leading a victory parade. Thousands marched while thousands more lined the pavements cheering and singing. Donnelly was in an open carriage drawn by four white horses, with his mother, a rather ample woman, sitting by his side. When the victory parade reached James' Street (it had taken seventeen days to do so, as it stopped at every public house en route from the Curragh) his mother stripped down to her waist, and slapping her bosoms she repeatedly called out: 'I am the woman who reared him and these are the breasts that fed him.'

For the next five years, Dan lived a full and sometimes desperate life. He died penniless at the early age of thirty-two on 18 February 1820. His funeral cortège was enormous, with thousands of his grief-stricken admirers lining the route and carriages and carts loaded with flowers forlornly following the hearse. A pair of boxing gloves belonging to him were carried on a silken cushion.

Dan Donnelly's body, having been laid to rest in Bully's Acre, was not destined to remain undisturbed – within days it had been stolen by medical students (an act which instigated riots). It was subsequently purchased from the grave robbers by an eminent Dublin surgeon called Hall, who had the right arm removed to study the muscle structure, and then respectfully reburied the body in Bully's Acre.

Surgeon Hall transported the arm to Scotland where it was disinfected, lacquered and used in anatomy lessons at the University of Edinburgh's medical college. It next appeared as an exhibit in an English travelling circus. Donnelly's arm returned to Ireland in 1904 when Hugh 'Texas' McAlevey, a Belfast bookmaker and bartender, acquired it to put on display at his bar, before relegating it to the attic of his betting parlour.

In 1953 James Byrne, the proprietor of the Hideout Olde World Pub in Kilcullen, County Kildare, was presented with it by a wine merchant who had purchased it just for fun. This was where the mummified arm was showcased for the next forty-three years. Desmond Byrne, son of the late James and current owner of Donnelly's arm, removed it from public viewing in 1996, when he sold the Hideout, and its whereabouts today are unknown.

Bully's Acre closed to the public after the cholera epidemic of 1832 when 3,200 victims were buried there within a year.

~ DANIEL O'CONNELL ~

'My body to Ireland, my heart to Rome and my soul to heaven.' So uttered the Great Liberator, Daniel O'Connell, to his servant Duggan, as he lay on his deathbed in Genoa in 1847. Taking him quite literally, following his death on 15 May, his heart was duly placed in a silver urn and sent to the Irish College in Rome, while his body was returned home.

When the Dublin Cemeteries Committee heard of their founder's death, they immediately took charge of what turned out to be one of the largest funerals ever seen in Dublin. Matthias O'Kelly, secretary of the Board of Glasnevin, left Ireland for Genoa charged with guarding the embalmed corpse and escorting it back to Dublin.[4] At 11.30 a.m. on Monday 2 August, the body arrived in Dublin on board the *Duchess of Kent*, where a small chapel of black cloth had been erected on deck. Thousands lined the streets in silence as a procession led by a group of silent boys from a Christian Brothers' school removed the body to Dublin's Pro-Cathedral.

O'Connell's remains lay in state for three days until the funeral on 5 August. For hours before the time appointed for the procession, every street leading to the church had a stream of men, women and children thronging towards the points from which the event could be seen. Great numbers

---

4   The Dublin Cemeteries Committee governs the cemetery, a voluntary not-for-profit body originally established by Daniel O'Connell in 1828. The committee was subsequently re-established under the Dublin Cemeteries Committee Acts of 1846 and 1970.

The original O'Connell crypt before his removal to beneath the tower in 1869. *Courtesy of the National Library of Ireland*

had even taken the precaution to bivouac in the best spots a few days previously. Thousands had flocked into the city prompting the railways to schedule special trains.

The *Weekly Freeman's Journal* said, 'no sound was to be heard – all was silent unutterable sorrow; the stillness of death seemed to pervade the living mass, and even the dark and lowering appearance of the forenoon added in no inconsiderable degree to the general appearance of the desolation.'

O'Connell's coffin was carried on a bier drawn by six horses. The triumphal car on which O'Connell had stood after his release from prison followed,[5] accompanied by a long train of mourning coaches. A huge procession of all

5   Despite O'Connell's cancellation of a monster meeting at Tara in 1843 he was arrested, charged with conspiracy, and sentenced to a year's imprisonment and a fine of £2,000, although the House of Lords released him after three months.

the trades, confraternities, philanthropic societies, bishops, judges, barristers and merchants followed the cortège as it passed through the city. Ships along the River Liffey lowered their flags.

Daniel O'Connell was buried in what became known as the O'Connell Circle in Glasnevin Cemetery on 5 August 1847. A witness, describing the events in the *Illustrated London News* of 14 August 1847 wrote, 'Sublime Gregorian music rose from 400 voices; a grand procession was formed and moved slowly through the grounds; the robes of clergy and corporations intermingled their hues with the rich foliage of trees and flowers. Fifty thousand persons were there to honour the memory of O'Connell.'

Twenty-two years later, his remains were exhumed and on 14 May 1869 O'Connell was reinterred in a crypt beneath an Irish round tower, specially built to house the coffin. While the original outer coffin was found to have deteriorated significantly, the mountings remained intact, and these were transferred to a new casket.

Daniel O'Connell's sarcophagus. *Courtesy of the Glasnevin Trust Collection*

The coffin was placed in a sarcophagus covered in a single slab of Kilkenny marble, nine feet by four. Three trefoil side panels allow the coffin to be seen. Inscriptions around the walls of the crypt read: 'My body to Ireland, My heart to Rome, My Soul to Heaven'; 'The Liberator of his Country'; 'The Friend of Civil and Religious Liberty all over the world'; and 'The Emancipator of his Catholic Fellow Subjects'.

O'Connell's heart rested in the Irish College in Rome until 1905 when, upon investigation, it appeared to have been lost. It has never been recovered.

~: ÉAMON DE VALERA :~

On 2 September 1975 a man who was sentenced to death almost sixty years earlier, Éamon de Valera, was buried in Glasnevin Cemetery.

By ten o'clock in the morning, the old men and women of the republican movement were gathered in the cemetery, to pay their last respects to 'The Chief'. Amongst them were Michael Vincent Merriman, Liam Kavanagh and Jim Dempsey of de Valera's Boland's Mill garrison, as well as Jimmy Kenny of the GPO garrison, who had later become a garda and a bodyguard to President de Valera. When Jim Dempsey, who had also been present when O'Donovan Rossa was buried, was asked how many of the 160 men of Boland's Mill garrison were still alive, he replied, 'Twenty-seven.'

Thousands of people, half of them children, waited for three hours outside the cemetery to catch a glimpse of de Valera's final 200-yard journey to his grave. One hundred men of the Old IRA's Eastern Command stood by the pavement from 11 a.m. and, as the warm summer sun beat down, one collapsed and had to be taken away.

'The Croppy Boy', played by the Army No. 1 Band, announced the coffin's approach to the cemetery. Twenty-one guns sent startled birds into the air as Commandant Tom Ryan ordered a salute from a piece of empty ground facing the cemetery gates. The coffin, placed on a gun carriage, was followed by four army jeeps laden with wreaths.

There was a slow applause as the coffin, draped in a

De Valera's grave. *Courtesy of the Glasnevin Trust Collection*

De Valera's funeral, 1975. *Courtesy of the Glasnevin Trust Collection*

Tricolour, passed through the gates of Glasnevin Cemetery, and on through a guard of infantry under Commandant Tom McGrath. De Valera's family stood to the right of the grave, although his grandson, Rev. Shan Ó Cúiv, joined the other priests on the left. Citizens, politicians and the curious, closed in rapidly behind the family and, for a few moments, there was an undignified scuffle to get the best view. People perched on the heads of statues and on high Celtic crosses. The old men and women of the republican movement, who had waited for three hours, did not succeed in approaching the grave at all.

A firing party of cadets, under Lieutenant Con McNamara, fired three volleys over the grave. Trumpeters and drummers from the band of the Western Command at Athlone sounded the 'Last Post' and 'Reveille'. Rev. Patrick Farnon led the prayers *as Gaeilge* and then Rev. Ó Cúiv said the Angelus.

As the dignitaries of church and state, the diplomats and the army moved away, it was the turn of the ordinary people to come close to the grave and say a final farewell to Éamon de Valera: Gaelic Leaguer, Volunteer Officer, condemned prisoner, Civil War anti-Treaty leader, President of Dáil Éireann, Taoiseach and Uachtarán na hÉireann.

∾ FRANK RYAN ∾

Frank Ryan once said, 'Isn't politics a dirty game? All the rattling of dead men's bones in a cause for which they never fought – all to no avail.'

Frank Ryan was born near Elton, County Limerick, and was educated at St Colman's College, Fermoy, and University College Dublin. His university career was interrupted in 1922 by service on the anti-Treaty side during the Civil War and a subsequent year's internment.

In 1931 Ryan helped to organise the radical left-wing, political, IRA-backed Saor Éire movement. However, by 1934, believing that republicanism without democracy meant fascism, Ryan broke with the IRA in an effort to build a united front against fascism in Ireland.

Frank Ryan in Spain. *Courtesy of the Glasnevin Trust Collection*

Commemoration at the grave of Frank Ryan on the tenth anniversary of his death in 1954. Members of the International Brigade travelled to East Germany to place flowers on his grave in Dresden.
Courtesy of the Glasnevin Trust Collection

In 1936 Ryan led a contingent of 200 Irishmen to Spain to fight in the 15th (International) Brigade for the Republic against General Franco's forces. He reached the rank of major, but was wounded early in 1937 and sent home to recuperate. On his return to Spain, he was appointed brigade adjutant to General José Miaja, commander of the Republican Army. He was captured by Italian forces in April 1938 and sentenced to death. De Valera, then Taoiseach, appealed at once to Franco for clemency and a nationwide campaign supported his appeal. Ryan's sentence was commuted to thirty year's imprisonment. A year later, by arrangement between the Irish, Spanish and German governments, he was set free and taken to Berlin.

In Berlin he met Seán Russell, chief of staff of the IRA, and left with him for Ireland in a German submarine. Russell died on board from peritonitis, and Ryan returned to Berlin, where German military intelligence treated him as a non-party neutral. Weakened by years of imprisonment, Ryan died from pleurisy and pneumonia at a hospital in Dresden in June 1944.

On hearing of his death, groups from across the political spectrum began campaigns to have his remains returned to Ireland. A republican-backed attempt by the Irish German Society was blocked by Irish communists, who in turn were blocked by Ryan's sister Eilis. In a letter, penned to the Irish government, she stated that she was anxious her brother's remains would 'not be used by people to boost a cause that Frank never favoured during his lifetime'.

Eventually in 1979, after intervention by the then TD Niall Andrews, the body was repatriated from East Germany. Three volunteers from the International Brigade – Frank Edwards, Peter O'Connor and Michael O'Riordan – travelled to East Germany to provide a guard of honour.

On 21 June 1979, Ryan's remains arrived at Whitefriar Street church, his local parish when he was in Dublin. The church was packed with all shades of republican and left-wing opinion, as well as those from his past, and ex-comrades and sympathisers from all over the world.

The cortège, on its way to Glasnevin Cemetery, halted at the GPO in memory of the dead of 1916. Frank's coffin was borne to his grave by the three men who had provided his guard of honour along with another Irish veteran of the Spanish Civil War, Terry Flanagan. Republican Con Lehane delivered the funeral oration while a piper played 'Limerick's Lamentation'.

A commemoration by the veterans of the International Brigade takes place every year at Ryan's graveside in Glasnevin Cemetery. Eoin O'Duffy, another Irishman who fought in Spain, but on the opposite side to Frank Ryan, is buried very close by.

~: GRAVE ROBBERS :~

The walls and towers surrounding Glasnevin Cemetery may look decorative, but in fact they served a grim purpose. They were built to guard against an epidemic of grave robbing, a grisly trade in early nineteenth-century Dublin.

Dublin anatomy schools and the Royal College of Surgeons required vast numbers of bodies to dissect in order to improve their scientific knowledge. Until the passing of the Anatomy Act of 1832, however, the supply of corpses was restricted to those of criminals sentenced to 'hanging and dissection'. There simply were not enough bodies to satisfy the medicos, creating a very lucrative prospect for the less discerning nineteenth-century Dublin entrepreneurs. Adult human remains fetched £2, while children's bodies were sold by the imperial inch – six shillings for the first twelve inches and nine pennies per inch for the remainder.

Following a daylight saunter through the cemetery to stake out their unfortunate prey, the grave robbers would return in the dead of night, armed with the tools of their trade: a wooden shovel for silent digging, a few ropes with hooks and a couple of sacks. The grave robbers worked from behind the headstone in an attempt to ensure that their gruesome doings might go unobserved by grieving relatives. Upon reaching the coffin they would prise it open, nimbly work the hook around the neck and slowly pull the corpse to the surface. The soil, which had been placed on the sacks, was easily returned to dispel suspicions. The body, once 'exhumed', was then put in a sack – hence the dreaded

Nineteenth-century depictions of grave robbers at work.
Courtesy of the Glasnevin Trust Collection

term 'Sack'em-ups' – and removed in a waiting cart. Leaving little to chance, their horses were shod in leather-covered shoes – an 'equine silencer' for a perfect getaway.

For rather obvious reasons, Irish grave robbers became known as 'The Resurrectionists', and such was their proficiency that they established a thriving export business, often dispatching the bodies in casks labelled 'Irish Cheese'.

Cemeteries employed various methods in a bid to thwart grave robbers, including adding straw to the soil which made digging difficult, placing heavy stone slabs over the grave, installing cages around the grave, paying watchmen and erecting walls and watch towers. So profound was the public's fear of grave robbing that, upon its opening, Prospect (Glasnevin) Cemetery erected a mobile watchtower that could be moved around as fresh graves were dug. Armed men would man the tower and the cemetery records have countless examples of them discharging their weapons. Later, in 1842, watchtowers were erected strategically around the perimeter walls and watchmen with guard dogs were employed.

As cemeteries became better guarded, some 'Resurrectionists' turned to murder to supply the anatomists with cadavers. The most infamous of these men were William Hare and William Burke who committed their crimes in Edinburgh in 1828. Only Burke was convicted of the crimes and was executed at the end of 1828. (Ironically, his body was turned over to an anatomist for public dissection.) Similar crimes were reported in several Irish towns and cities. Public outrage eventually forced legislators to pass the British 1832 Anatomy Act, which provided anatomists with a legal source of cadavers. Once these laws were in place, grave robbing quickly declined.

∾ EOIN O'DUFFY ∾

Can a march to a cemetery to commemorate the dead lead
to the overthrow of a government? Well Éamon de Valera
thought it could and perhaps so too did Eoin O'Duffy.

Eoin O'Duffy was born in County Monaghan on
20 October 1892. In 1917 he joined the Irish Volunteers
and played an active role in the War of Independence. He
became director of organisation of the IRA in 1921 and was
appointed chief of staff in January 1922, a position he left
in July with the outbreak of the Civil War. He supported
the Anglo-Irish Treaty of December 1921 and served as a
general in the Free State army. When the Civil War ended
in 1923 O'Duffy was appointed commissioner of an Garda
Síochána.

In 1933 he became the chief of the right-wing political
organisation the Army Comrades Association and changed
its name to the National Guard. His organisation adopted
the symbols of fascism and a distinctive blue uniform. The
group became known as the Blueshirts and were an active
rallying force for opponents of Fianna Fáil.

In August 1933 O'Duffy was in the midst of planning
a parade of Blueshirts to march to Glasnevin Cemetery to
commemorate the deaths, eleven years previously, of Michael
Collins and Arthur Griffith. Remembering Mussolini's
march on Rome, and fearing a *coup d'état*, de Valera promptly
banned the parade. Decades later, he said he was unsure as
to whether the Irish army would obey his orders to suppress
the perceived threat, or if the soldiers would support the

Eoin O'Duffy. *Courtesy of the Glasnevin Trust Collection*

Blueshirts (who included many ex-soldiers). O'Duffy accepted the ban and insisted that he was committed to upholding the law. Instead, several provincial parades took place to commemorate the deaths of Griffith and Collins.

De Valera saw this move as defying his ban, and the National Guard was declared illegal.

That same month, O'Duffy made his mark on history, when his Blueshirt movement joined Cosgrave's Cumann na nGaedheal party and the National Centre Party, to form Fine Gael, the United Ireland Party. O'Duffy was appointed its first leader, even though he was not a TD at the time. In September 1934, O'Duffy resigned as Fine Gael leader.

By 1936 a new military adventure beckoned O'Duffy, with the Spanish Civil War offering him a chance to help one of his fascist friends, General Francisco Franco in Spain. Despite de Valera's government ruling that participation in the Spanish conflict was illegal, O'Duffy was able to rally 700 of his followers to form an Irish brigade to fight on Franco's side. The group did not acquit themselves well and were once fired upon accidentally by Franco's troops, after which they returned to Ireland.

Upon his return from Spain, O'Duffy retired from politics. He approached the German Legation in Dublin in the summer of 1943, with an offer to organise an Irish Volunteer Legion to help with the German war effort on the Russian front. However, the Germans decided not to take O'Duffy up on his offer.

O'Duffy's health had begun to deteriorate by this time and he died in the Pembroke Nursing Home in Dublin on 30 November 1944 at the age of fifty-two. Despite their earlier differences, he was given a state funeral by the government. Following a requiem mass at Dublin's pro-cathedral, O'Duffy was buried at Glasnevin Cemetery, not far from Frank Ryan, an Irish adversary in the Spanish Civil War.

⌁ RICHARD COLEMAN ⌁

Born in 1890 in Swords, County Dublin, Richard Coleman was one of eleven siblings, most of whom were active in the Gaelic League founded by Douglas Hyde in 1893 to promote the Gaelic revival and the Irish language. Coleman's father was a teacher in the Swords New Borough Male School on Seatown Road, which Richard attended before going to O'Connell's CBS on North Richmond Street, Dublin. When he finished school he joined the Christian Brothers, but left after four years, and ended up working in Swords for the Prudential Insurance Company.

When Thomas MacDonagh came to Swords to recruit for the recently formed Irish Volunteers in April 1914,

Richard Coleman (*third from right in the second row from front, kneeling*) with released prisoners at the Mansion House, 1917.
Courtesy of Kilmainham Gaol Museum

Richard was among the first to sign up. When the leader of the Volunteers John Redmond decided to support the British war effort and a split in the Volunteers ensued later that year, the members of the Fingal Battalion who rejected Redmond's position elected Richard as their new captain.

On Easter Sunday 1916, Richard mobilised the battalion and prepared them for the following day. On Easter Monday they, along with other Volunteers from surrounding areas, came under the direction of Thomas Ashe, whose instructions were to prevent British reinforcements from reaching Dublin.

On Tuesday, Thomas Ashe was asked by James Connolly to send forty men to Dublin city, but Ashe decided to send twenty and the remainder fought at the Battle of Ashbourne under the command of Frank Lawless. Richard Coleman went with the GPO contingent and on reaching the GPO, the group was split into two. Six men became the tunnelling unit around the GPO, 'the engineering corps', while the others, under Richard, were instructed to reinforce the garrison under Seán Heuston in the Mendicity Institution.

Connolly's parting words to them did not augur well for their mission: 'I don't think you will all get there, but get as far as you can.' However, they got as far as the Mendicity Institution unscathed.

The Mendicity garrison, under intensive fire, surrendered on Thursday. Richard and his comrades were marched to the Rotunda Hospital for identification purposes. Richard was court-martialled and sentenced to death, but this was commuted to three years' penal servitude. He was sent to

Patriæ suæ amore, Vinctus et Exul,

RICHARDUS COLEMAN,

Emigravit ad Patriam veram

Quinto ante Idus Decembres

1918.

Det ei Pater vitam sine termino

In Patria.

FATHER KNIGHT.

A Prisoner and an Exile

For love of his native land

RICHARD COLEMAN,

Passed to his true country

9th December, 1918.

May his Father grant him life without end

In his real homeland.

FATHER KNIGHT.

A mass card for Richard Coleman, 1918. These cards were produced by the Prisoners' Dependants' Fund, who used the monies raised in their sale to look after the families of those interred.
Courtesy of Kilmainham Gaol Museum

Dartmoor and then to Lewes Prison, but was released under the General Amnesty of 1917.

Like many released prisoners, Richard campaigned for Éamon de Valera in the Clare by-election in 1918, which resulted in his arrest and imprisonment in Mountjoy Jail. He went on hunger strike and, after the death of Thomas Ashe, was transferred to Cork Jail and then to Dundalk. He began another hunger strike in Dundalk, and was released shortly afterwards.

He was soon rearrested, along with others, as part of the British authorities' 'German Plot' conspiracy, where they accused the IRA of conspiring with the Germans to start another rebellion in Ireland. The prisoners were assembled first in Dublin Castle on 17 May 1918 and then sent to Usk and Gloucester jails in Britain.

Richard and his fellow prisoners were ordered to wear prison uniforms, but they resisted and, at the direction of the home office, the prison governor, Young, capitulated. On their first night in Usk, the internees won the right to free association, the right to receive and send letters, to smoke and to wear their own clothes.

Despite their victory, the prison regime weakened the men and, with the onset of a severe winter, many succumbed to the influenza virus, which had already reached epidemic proportions, killing hundreds outside the prison walls. Richard was among a group of POWs struck down by the virus. They were left in their damp and cold cells for three days after they were infected. On 1 December a new prison doctor, Dr Morton, was appointed and he immediately diagnosed that Richard was suffering from pneumonia and had him transferred to hospital. Sadly it was too little too late and he died a few days later, on 9 December 1918.

Richard Coleman's remains were released to his brother and taken to Dublin where they lay in state for a week in St Andrew's Church, Westland Row. Over 100,000 people filed past the coffin to pay their last respects. Volunteers in uniform formed a guard of honour.

A public funeral procession in driving rain from Westland Row to Glasnevin was followed by over 15,000 people. Three volleys of shots were fired over the grave at the Republican Plot in Glasnevin Cemetery where Richard was laid to rest.

~: FENIAN GRAVES :~

The Fenians were the first to use funerals for propaganda purposes, and the burial of Terence Bellew MacManus gave them the perfect template.

Terence Bellew MacManus was born in Tempo, County Fermanagh, in 1811. At a young age he moved to Liverpool, where he worked successfully as a shipping agent. In 1843 he returned to Ireland and joined the Young Ireland movement, a political, cultural and social movement which made Irish nationalism a political force in Irish society. MacManus threw himself enthusiastically into the revolutionary group.

In 1848 Ireland was still suffering from the Great Famine. Popular uprisings were breaking out across Europe, governments and monarchs were toppling, and Young Ireland leaders, including William Martin O'Brien, John Blake Dillon and John O'Mahony, were planning a rebellion for July 1848 in Ballingarry, County Tipperary. MacManus was an ardent participant.

However, the rising failed and MacManus was arrested in Cork as he tried to board a ship for America. He was tried for high treason and condemned to death. His sentence was later commuted to penal servitude and he was shipped to Van Diemen's Land (Tasmania) on board the HMS *Swift*. In 1852 he escaped and settled in California, where he attempted in vain to revive his former shipping agency. MacManus died in poverty on 15 January 1861.

The Fenian movement, which was gathering strength and popularity in Ireland and America, recognised the

Young Ireland monument by Sir Thomas Farrell, RA.
Courtesy of the Glasnevin Trust Collection

propaganda potential that presented itself in the death of this former rebel. The remains of MacManus were transported across the United States, arriving in St Patrick's Cathedral in New York for a requiem mass. At each stop along the way, great rallies were held, both to publicise the nationalist cause in Ireland and to raise funds.

It took nearly eleven months before the coffin bearing Terence Bellew MacManus arrived in Cork, where hundreds of thousands gathered to meet the casket. A ship flying the English flag was passing along the quay, and a little boy

William Smith O'Brien.

Michael Doheny.

T. B. MacManus.

Patrick O'Donohoe.

T. Devin Reilly.

Richard O'Gorman, Junior.

John Savage.

Young Irelanders. *Courtesy of the Glasnevin Trust Collection*

caused a commotion by jumping aboard, clambering up the ropes and tearing the flag down.

By nightfall the coffin was placed on board a train for Dublin, along with the delegation of chief mourners. They were armed with pistols, as it was rumoured that there might be some necessity for using them. It seems some men were in favour of using the occasion as the spark to ignite another rising, believing it would rouse the country if the remains were taken to Slievenamon, or some such historic place.

En route between Cork and Dublin, when the train pulled in to Limerick Junction, a large crowd had gathered on the platform and it was believed that, if an attempt was to be made, then this would be the most likely place. James Stephens had previously given orders that the men of Tipperary town be there to prevent the body being removed. As the bell rang for the train to depart, Stephens called on the men to kneel down and say a 'Pater' and an 'Ave' for the dead, and, while the whole crowd was on their knees, the train moved out.

On its arrival in Dublin, Archbishop Cullen, who condemned the ecumenical Young Ireland movement of 1848 and opposed the Fenian movement, supporting redress by constitutional means, refused to allow the remains to lie in state in any church in his diocese, except for the funeral mass. So the funeral ceremony took place at the Mechanics Institute, Lower Abbey Street (later the site of the Abbey Theatre), and then the funeral procession moved on to Glasnevin, where James Stephens gave a candlelight oration.

Other Fenians buried in the same plot are John O'Mahony (Young Irelander and Fenian), Charles Patrick McCarthy (Irish Republican Brotherhood), Daniel Reddin (Irish Republican Brotherhood), Patrick Nally (Irish Republican Brotherhood) and James Stritch (Irish Republican Brotherhood).

ᔰ CHRISTY BROWN ᔰ

When the author, poet and artist Christy Brown died in 1981, another Dublin author, Christopher Nolan, penned the following lines:

Firstly, may I say Christy Brown,
I loudly laud you for pioneering
Nasty niches of poisonous terrain
In your search for an escape route
For brain-damaged Man.
I nobly salute
Nature's Noblesse of creativity
As expressed in your lyrical musings.
Regretfully we never met
But memory of nodding acquaintance
With savage, pathetic Man's
Indifference to our common plight
Coupled with dank death's call to you
On my Birthday,
Makes brothers of two anointed ones.

(*Reproduced with the permission of Curtis Brown Group
Ltd, London, on behalf of the Estate of Christopher Nolan.*
© *Christopher Nolan, 1981*)

Christy Brown was born in Crumlin, Dublin, in 1932. The son of a bricklayer, Christy was one of thirteen surviving children. He suffered from severe cerebral palsy and was incapable for years of deliberate movement or speech.

However, his mother Bridget continued to speak to him, work with him and teach him, until he famously snatched a piece of chalk from his sister with his left foot to make a mark on the floor. By the age of five Christy had gained considerable control over his left foot and, seizing the opportunity, his mother taught him the alphabet which he laboriously copied holding the chalk between his left toes. Gradually Christy learned to spell out words, enabling him to read.

During her twenty-first child's birth, when Christy was in his teens, Bridget met a lady almoner (an early type of social worker) who worked in the impoverished areas of Dublin with an Irish doctor-cum-writer named Robert Collis. The lady almoner told Dr Collis about Christy. Collis met with Christy in the Brown family home in Kimmage and used his contacts in the London Hospital to diagnose Christy with the disease known as 'double-athetoid cerebral palsy'. This encounter prompted Collis to establish a treatment centre for all cerebral palsy victims in Ireland.

Christy Brown at work.
© *Getty images*

Collis and Christy established a lifelong friendship based on their common love for literature. Collis, who was close to established Irish writers like Cecil Day-Lewis and Frank O'Connor, not only provided Christy with introductions to these great authors, but also played a pivotal role in inspiring Christy to write. With the encouragement of Dr Collis, Christy completed his first book, an autobiography, entitled *My Left Foot*.

My Left Foot was later expanded into the novel *Down All The Days* which went on to become an international best-seller, with translations in many languages. *Down All The Days* was followed by a series of other novels, including *A Shadow on Summer*. Christy also published a number of poetry collections, including *Come Softly to My Wake*.

On 5 October 1972 Christy married his nurse, Mary Carr, in Sutton, County Dublin. The couple settled first in Ballyheigue, County Kerry, and then moved to Parbrook, Somerset, in England. Christy died at age forty-nine, on 7 September 1981, having choked while eating.

On a day of drizzling rain and overcast skies, Christy Brown was laid to rest in his native Dublin, following mass at St Bernadette's Church, Clogher Road, the parish where Christy and another famous Dublin writer, Brendan Behan, had grown up.

There had been some confusion with regards to the arrangements, with many people thinking the funeral was to be a day later, and so only a modest crowd attended. Christy's wife Mary was delayed in a derailed train in Portlaoise and the service proceeded without her. A little girl, with a strong Dublin accent, sang 'Going Home' to the congregation. Alas,

due to another mix-up, Christy's coffin was not present, as it had been left in a funeral parlour in Thomas Street.

After the mass the mourners went to collect the coffin in Thomas Street and took to a local pub to await Mary's arrival.

An hour and a half later, following a police escort, the funeral procession finally arrived at Glasnevin Cemetery. The gravediggers, who had waited for hours, had now gone on their break, and more time was wasted waiting for their return. Eventually they arrived and Christy Brown was finally laid to rest.

Christie Browne's grave.
Courtesy of David Cleary,
Glasnevin Trust Collection

∿ GRAVEYARD SYMBOLS ∿

Were you ever told as a child not to step on a grave because you might wake the dead? Or told by your friends to hold your breath as you passed a cemetery? Well these, and many other customs and superstitions around death, have passed down to us from pagan times and many have a simple explanation.

Black mourning clothing, now worn as a mark of respect, was originally used as a disguise – to hide the wearer's identity from returning spirits. Pagans believed that returning spirits would fail to recognise them in their new attire, and would be confused and overlook them.

Shutting the eyes of the deceased was believed to prevent the corpse from being able to choose someone to accompany him to the grave. Often pennies were used to hold the lids down. Holding your breath while passing a cemetery and covering the face of the deceased with a sheet comes from the pagan belief that the spirit of the deceased escaped through the mouth.

In some cultures, the home of the deceased was burned or destroyed to keep his spirit from returning; in others the doors were unlocked and windows were opened to ensure that the soul was able to escape.

In nineteenth-century Dublin, the dead were carried out of the house feet first, to prevent the spirit from looking back into the house and beckoning another member of the family to follow them. Mirrors in the house were covered in a black crepe material so the soul of the departed would not be trapped behind the glass and prevented from passing to 'the other side'. Curtains would be drawn and clocks would be stopped at the time of death. Stopping time was believed to allow the spirit to move on.

The body was watched over every minute until burial, hence the custom of 'waking'. The wake also served as a safeguard from burying someone who was not actually dead, but in a coma, which in Victorian times was a major concern. There were many patented inventions created at the time to thwart this eventuality, including coffins fitted up with bells and glass windows, as well as tongue-pulling devices. The practical reason for most wakes lasting up to three or four days was to allow relatives to arrive from far away.

The use of flowers and candles helped hide unpleasant odours before embalming became common. Family photographs were turned face down to prevent any of the close relatives and friends of the deceased being possessed by the spirit of the dead. Funeral music had its origin in ancient chants designed to placate the spirits.

Some other cultures took their fear of the departed to extremes. The Saxons cut off the feet of their dead so that the corpse would be unable to walk. Some aboriginal tribes took the extreme step of cutting off the head of the dead, believing this would leave spirits too busy searching for their head to worry about the living!

Cemeteries are home to some of the most unusual rituals to ward off the spirits. The use of tombstones may go back to the belief that ghosts could be weighed down. Mazes found at the entrance to many ancient tombs were thought to have been constructed to keep the deceased from returning to

The Ouroboros symbol used on Celtic crosses represents cyclicality or
the eternal return.
Courtesy of the Glasnevin Trust Collection

the world as a spirit, since it was believed that ghosts could only travel in straight lines. Some people even insisted that the funeral procession should return from the graveside by a different path to the one taken there, so that the departed's ghost wouldn't be able to follow them home.

Some of the rituals, which we now practise as a sign of respect for the deceased, may also be rooted in fear of the spirits. Beating on the grave, the firing of guns, funeral bells, and wailing chants were all used by pagan cultures to scare away ghosts or spirits at the cemetery.

In many cemeteries, the vast majority of graves are oriented in such a manner that the bodies lie with their heads to the west and their feet to the east. This very old custom originates with the pagan sun worshippers, but is primarily attributed to Christians who believe that the final summons to judgement will come from the east.

∾ JOHN PHILPOT CURRAN ∾

'My dear doctor, I am surprised to hear you say that I am coughing very badly, as I have been practising all night', were apparently some of the last recorded words of John Philpot Curran.

Born in Newmarket, County Cork, Curran was educated in Trinity College Dublin and the Middle Temple, London. In 1783 he was given a seat in the House of Commons for Kilbeggan, County Westmeath, but, refusing to be subject to his patron's views, he bought another seat (at his own expense) for Rathcormack, County Cork, which he held until 1797. In parliament, he was a strong advocate of Catholic emancipation and a severe critic of patronage and corruption. (In the eighteenth and nineteenth century seats were not linked to population but to boroughs and it was very easy for the local landowner to control who his tenants voted for, as elections were done in the open with a show of hands. For example, in 1812 the Duke of Bedford sold the borough of Camelford with its constituency of only thirty-one voters to the Earl of Darlington for £32,000.)

Curran defended the United Irishmen

John Philpot Curran.
Courtesy of the Glasnevin Trust Collection

Hamilton Rowen in 1794 and Wolfe Tone after the 1798 rebellion. He also opposed the Act of Union with vigour, but despite his support for the nationalist cause, when he discovered that his daughter was secretly engaged to the republican leader Robert Emmet, Curran was horrified. He tried to split them up, and behaved so badly towards her that she had to leave the family home at Grange Road, Rathfarnham. His daughter's relationship with Emmet, executed for treason in 1803, caused him great difficulty. The authorities suspected that Curran was involved with the rebels, but he was completely exonerated of the charge.

Having been appointed master of the rolls in Ireland in 1806, he retired in 1814 and moved to London. Curran had married his cousin Sarah Creagh, but in London his wife left him for another man.

John Philpot Curran died at his home in Brompton in October 1817. His funeral in Paddington was attended by, amongst others, the singer-songwriter, Thomas Moore. He was buried in London, but it was said that his dying wish was to be interred in Ireland. When the Dublin Cemeteries Committee met in 1833 it was decided that the burial of Curran, in the newly opened Prospect Cemetery in Glasnevin, would be very fitting. They wrote to Curran's son, John, and received his blessing.

An employee, John Graham, was sent to London to secure the remains. Curran's corpse arrived in Dublin on a very wet and stormy night in 1834 and was brought to Glasnevin cemetery by torchlight. Recalling the events, Graham wrote:

It was on a very gloomy day of November that the remains were removed with strict privacy to Dublin. Towards night, and as we arrived in the metropolis, the weather was marked with peculiar severity: the rain fell in torrents, and a violent storm howled, whilst the darkness was relieved occasionally by vivid lightning, accompanied by peals of thunder. This added much to the solemnity of the scene as we passed slowly through the streets, from which the violence of the night had driven almost all persons. As we approached the cemetery, where groups of workmen, by the aid of torches, were engaged in making the necessary preparations for the deposit of the remains, the scene became most impressive and effecting; and, after a brief period of delay, during which all around stood with uncovered heads as the body of the great Irishman was lowered to its place of final repose, the scene was marked by every feature of a grand and impressive picture of devotion.

Sculpted by John Hogan, the sarcophagus in which Curran rests was modelled on that of Scipio Barbatus in Rome. It stands at eight feet two inches high, and is composed of fine Irish granite, each block weighing from four to five tons. The sum of £300 had been set apart to pay for the tomb, the balance of which paid for a bust of Curran, carved by Christopher Moore, which is in St Patrick's Cathedral, Dublin.

John Philpot Curran's grave. *Courtesy of the Glasnevin Trust Collection*

⤳ CHARGE OF THE LIGHT BRIGADE ⤳

Someone had blunder'd:
Theirs not to make reply,
Theirs not to reason why,
Theirs but to do and die:
Into the valley of Death
Rode the six hundred.

Alfred, Lord Tennyson

Now Tennyson was a fine poet but he wasn't that great at counting. In fact 673 men rode in the Charge of the Light Brigade – a disastrous charge of British cavalry against Russian forces during the Crimean War (1853–56) – and of these 114 were Irish. On 25 October 1854, during the Battle of Balaclava, a misunderstood order sent three regiments of cavalrymen, led by Lord Cardigan, thundering up a valley into heavy Russian gunfire. During the charge 118 (including twenty-one Irishmen) were killed and 127 (including sixteen Irish) wounded – their graves can be found all over Dublin.

One of the unsung wounded was James Devlin, whose lonely grave lies in Glasnevin Cemetery. James Salamander Devlin was born on board a naval gunboat (women often sailed on these ships) called the *Salamander* in 1834 and, according to the custom of those born at sea, was named after the ship.

On 8 February 1850, at the age of sixteen, he enlisted in the British army at Athlone, where his father was the governor of the jail. After enlistment, he served with the 4th Light Dragoons in Dublin's Phoenix Park before being sent

The Charge of the Light Brigade entered into every aspect of public life as demonstrated by this music from 1896.
Courtesy of the Glasnevin Trust Collection

to the Crimea. The wounds he received during that fateful charge at Balaclava meant that it was his first and last military

An artist's impression of the Charge of the Light Brigade, 1854.
Courtesy of the Glasnevin Trust Collection

action. His sword hand was almost severed by a Russian sabre cut and his left shoulder was smashed by a musket bullet. The bullet was extracted by an army surgeon with a pair of pliers. However, a few decades later inflammation re-opened the wound and it did not close until a piece of his jacket emerged, having been lodged in there for twenty-nine years.

After the battle he was awarded the Crimea Medal with three clasps, the Turkish Medal and the Medal for Distinguished Conduct in the Field.[6] He returned to Ireland an invalid and worked as the chief clerk in the adjutant-general's department in Dublin Castle. He died on 3 February 1892 at his residence, 8 Connaught Terrace, Garville Road, Rathgar, at fifty-eight years of age.

---

6   A clasp is added to the Crimea Medal for each recognised action or battle for which the regiment was present.

The Irish Times reported on the funeral in Glasnevin Cemetery by saying:

Amongst the many tributes of affection and sympathy may be mentioned a beautiful wreath sent by the officers of the 4th, as well as those sent by Mrs Sheeran, Major Gorman, Major Grace, and Miss Cort.

The coffin, which was of solid oak, bore on its breast plate the following inscription: 'James Devlin. Died 3rd February 1892. Aged 58 years. R.I.P.' The chief mourners were William Francis Devlin (son), Joseph H. Sheeran (brother-in-law) and James W. Dawson (nephew).

James Devlin's gravestone is a simple white marble cross, the inscription on which reads:

James Devlin, who died 3rd of February 1892, aged 58 years. 'One of the Noble Six Hundred.' Served with the 4th Queen's Own Light Dragoons in the Crimea and was severely wounded in the ever memorable Charge of the Light Brigade, 25th of October 1854.

At the base of the stone is 'Rest, Warrior, rest, heed not the route. Until the trumpet sounds the grand "Turn Out." R.I.P.'

The graveyards of Dublin are littered with tales of a rich military history. Men who lived, fought and died in wars across the old world and the new, in uniforms as varied as the landscapes in which they battled. James Devlin is just one of these.

~: ANNE DEVLIN :~

I've never liked the saying, 'behind every great man is a great woman', because, nine times out of ten, they are placed behind him in the history books that follow. Anne Devlin was one of these.

Anne Devlin, Ireland's first revolutionary woman, was born at Cronbeg, near Rathdrum, County Wicklow, in 1780. Her aunt was married to a man named Dwyer and was the mother of the Wicklow rebel Michael Dwyer. In 1800 the Devlin family moved to Dublin and Anne met Robert Emmet who was living in Butterfield Lane. Emmet was immersed in the planning of an uprising and many of his co-conspirators used his house on a regular basis for meetings or to gather arms. Emmet asked Anne to act as his housekeeper to convey an impression of normality. In this guise Anne acted as his adviser, messenger and agent.

On the evening of 23 July 1803 the rising commenced in Dublin, but despite taking the British authorities by surprise, the lack of co-

Anne Devlin.
Courtesy of Kilmainham Gaol Museum

ordination and confusion amongst the ranks led to its collapse after a night of bloody street clashes.

Anne and the rest of her family, including her eight-year-old sister, were arrested. Anne was interrogated and tortured to extract information about the whereabouts of Emmet and his cohorts. Despite being half hung with a noose around her neck, which was tied over a cart in the yard of Dublin Castle, she refused to speak.

She was brought before the infamous chief of police in Dublin, Major Sirr, who tried to bribe her, but again she refused to inform on her employer. Anne was sent to Kilmainham Gaol for further interrogation. By then Emmet had been arrested and when they met there briefly he urged her to inform on him to save herself as he was already doomed, but she refused. On 19 September 1803 Emmet was found guilty of high treason and sentenced to be hanged, drawn and quartered. The following day he was executed on Thomas Street, Dublin, and Anne was driven past the blood-stained block on her way to Dublin Castle for further interrogation.

She was kept in solitary confinement in Kilmainham Gaol in squalid conditions and was subjected to brutal treatment, but consistently refused to cooperate despite the fact that her entire family was also being held (they were mostly released in December 1803).

She was finally released in 1806. She earned a living by taking in washing and other work and later married a man named Campbell. For a few years Anne knew peace and love and was the mother of two children, a boy and a girl. Then her husband died in 1845, and Anne was once again left to fend for herself. It is not known what happened to her children.

She began a long-standing battle with hunger, want and poverty, which lasted for more than forty years. She was the same age as Emmet, but when Richard Robert Madden, an Irish doctor, writer, abolitionist and historian of the United Irishmen, discovered her and made known her story through his letters to the Young Irelanders, hardship and hunger had made her look ten years older. Madden travelled abroad from time to time, and in September 1851, on his return from a trip to the continent, he went to see how Anne Devlin was faring, but could find no trace of her. He kept on searching and the result of his efforts is described thus in a letter to the *Nation* newspaper of 27 September 1851:

> Last week, a gentleman who always took the warmest interest in this noble creature, was informed that she was still living in a miserable garret at No. 2 Little Elbow Lane, a squalid alley running from the Coombe to Pimlico. On this day week he sought that wretched abode; but she had died two days previously, and had been buried in Glasnevin on the preceding day.
>
> A young woman, with an ill-fed infant in her arms, apparently steeped in poverty, but kindly and well-mannered, in whose room Anne Devlin had lodged, said: 'The poor creature, God rest her, it's well for her – she's dead. There was a coffin got from the Society for her, and she was buried yesterday. She was very badly off, not only for food, but for bedclothes too.'

She was buried in an unpurchased grave in Glasnevin Cemetery with her husband, but although the cemetery has no record of this it appears that following the efforts of Doctor Madden she was exhumed and reinterred with a headstone which states:

Anne Devlin's grave. *Courtesy of the Glasnevin Trust Collection*

To the memory of Anne Devlin (Campbell)
The faithful servant of Robert Emmet
Who possessed some rare and many noble qualities
Who lived in obscurity and poverty, and so died on the
18th day of Sept 1851
Aged 70 years.

~: ZOZIMUS :~

Michael Moran was born in 1794 in Faddle Alley, off the Black Pits in Dublin's Liberties. At two weeks old he was blinded by illness but, despite this early setback, he developed an amazing ability to memorise verse.

Moran became a regular sight all over the Liberties,  making his living reciting poetry, much of which he composed himself. Taking his place alongside Dublin's street characters – Owny the Fool (who was as wise as an owl), Peg the Man and Fat Mary, Dublin's prima donna – Moran was nicknamed 'Zozimus', a reference from one of his popular recitations about the life, conversion and death of St Mary of Egypt, who was discovered in the wilderness by the pious Bishop Zozimus in the fifth century.

Michael 'Zozimus' Moran was described by a contemporary as being 'a tall, gaunt, blind man, dressed in a heavy, long-tailed coat and a dinged high hat, armed with a blackthorn stick secured to his wrist by a thong and finished by an iron ferule.'

Zozimus, the blind balladeer of the Liberties.
Courtesy of the Glasnevin Trust Collection

He began each performance with the verse:

Ye sons and daughters of Erin,
Gather round poor Zozimus, yer friend;
Listen boys, until yez hear
My charming song so dear

It is said that Zozimus only strayed outside the Liberties to entertain at runaway marriages, which were regularly performed at Cullenswood in Ranelagh by a rogue German clergyman named Schultz.

After years of performing on the streets of Dublin, Zozimus' voice began to fade. Losing his only means of livelihood he soon became feeble and bedridden. Zozimus died at home, in No. 14½ Patrick's Street, Dublin, on 3 April 1846. He had dictated directions for his funeral to Rev. Nicholas O'Farrell:

I have no coronet to go before me,
Nor bucephali-us that ever bore me;
But put my hat and stick and gloves together,
That bore for years the very worst of weather,
And rest assured in spirit will be there
May of A-gypt and Susannah fair.
And Pharaoh's daughter – with the heavenly blushes –
That took the drowning goslin from the rushes.
I'll not permit a tomb-stone stuck above me,
Nor effigy; but, boys, if still yees love me,
Build a nate house for all whose fate is hard,
And give a bed to every wandern' bard.

Grave robbers had been rife in Dublin in the early eighteenth century and although their activities had been curtailed by new laws, the fear of them still lingered, so Zozimus arranged to be buried in Glasnevin Cemetery, which had high walls and watchtowers and was guarded day and night.

The grave of Zozimus lay unmarked until the Dublin City Ramblers
erected a stone in 1988.
Courtesy of David Cleary, Glasnevin Trust Collection

A week after Zozimus died a miniature painter, Horatio Nelson of Grafton Street, produced a work entitled 'Zozimus, Rhymer and Reciter', the only known image of Michael Moran.

A short time later a man appeared on Patrick Street, dressed in a long-tailed coat and hat, and declared himself to be Zozimus. He went from pub to pub attempting to claim free whiskey but met with little success.

⁓ THE NEILAN BROTHERS ⁓

On the morning of 24 April 1916, two brothers awoke and dressed in their respective military tunics. That day they would both hold rifles and fire upon the enemy. They would both watch as the city of Dublin became a battleground and one of them would die in the uniform of the king of England while the other would hold out with the rebels until surrender came six days later.

On 7 June 1881 Gerald Neilan was born, the second son of John (of Ballygalda, Roscommon) and Eva (née Kelly) Neilan of 4 Mount Harold Terrace, Leinster Road, Dublin. Gerald's father was a farmer and local justice of the peace and his mother was the daughter of John Kelly of Essex Lawn, Roscommon.

Gerald was educated at Clongowes Wood College, County Kildare. A fellow schoolmate James Joyce would go on to confuse and entertain the world with his works *Ulysses* and *Finnegans Wake*.

In 1899 Gerald enlisted in the 2nd Battalion of the Derbyshire Regiment (The Sherwood Foresters) and after basic training he was sent to Malta. From there he was posted to South Africa where he saw action against the Boers. For his service he was awarded the Queen's South Africa Medal with clasps for Cape Colony, Orange Free State, Transvaal and South Africa 1902.

On 6 March 1902 he was wounded severely at Bushman's Kop and was posted to China to recuperate. From China he was posted to Malaysia, where he remained until he finished his eight-year contract as a corporal in 1907.

After leaving the army Gerald joined the Birmingham City police on Saturday 18 January 1908, serving on the 'D' Division with warrant number 7675, and was appointed to the ranks on Wednesday 27 January 1909. Gerald remained with the police until 20 December 1914, when he resigned to rejoin the army. He was immediately given a commission, being gazetted to the 24th Battalion, Northumberland Fusiliers. With this unit Gerald was given the job of musketry instructor.

On 4 February 1916 he was transferred to the Royal Dublin Fusiliers. On the morning of 24 April, the 10th Battalion, Royal Dublin Fusiliers, were training at the Royal Barracks in Dublin when the Easter Rising broke out. They were ordered to relieve Dublin Castle. As they made their way up the quays they came under heavy fire from the Mendicity Institution and Gerald Neilan was killed by a sniper bullet to the head.

Gerald's brother Arthur was born in 1895. He also attended Clongowes Wood College, where one of his fellow pupils was John Charles McQuaid, later Archbishop of Dublin and Primate of Ireland. In contrast to his brother Gerald, Arthur joined the Irish Volunteers when he turned eighteen. He was twenty-one years of age when the Rising broke out and was part of the Four Courts garrison under Ned Daly. After the rebels surrendered, he was transported to Knutsford Detention Barracks on 1 May 1916. He was released under a general amnesty in 1917 and returned to his mother's address at 4 Mount Harold Terrace.

Arthur served with the 4th Battalion, Dublin Brigade, in the War of Independence and the pro-Treaty Free State

Damage caused to the Four Courts during the 1916 Rising.
Courtesy of Mercier Archives

army during the Irish Civil War. He died on 24 November 1944 in the military hospital of St Bricans and his home address was given as Leinster Road. He was buried in the same grave in Glasnevin as his brother Gerald.

~: BIBLIOGRAPHY :~

Bateson, R. (2002) *Dead and Buried in Dublin: An illustrated guide to the historic graves of Dublin*. Meath: Irish Graves Publications

Bateson, R. (2004) *The End: An illustrated guide to the graves of Irish writers*. Meath: Irish Graves Publications

Bateson, R. (2010) *They Died by Pearse's Side*. Dublin: Irish Graves Publications

Boran, P. (2000) *A Short History of Dublin*. Cork: Mercier Press

Boylan, H. (ed.) (1998) *A Dictionary of Irish Biography*. Dublin: Gill & Macmillan Ltd

Burke, T. (2004) 'In Memory of Lieut. Tom Kettle 'B' Company, 9th Royal Dublin Fusiliers' in *Dublin Historical Record, LVII* (2)

Carey, T. (2000) *Mountjoy: The Story of a Prison*. Cork: The Collins Press

Clare, A. (2011) *Unlikely Rebels: The Gifford Girls and the Fight for Irish Freedom*. Cork: Mercier Press

Collins, M. (2011) *The Path to Freedom: Articles and Speeches*. Cork: Mercier Press

Connell, C. (2004) *Glasnevin Cemetery, Dublin, 1832–1900*. Dublin: Four Courts Press Ltd

Connell, J. E. A. (2006) *Where's Where in Dublin: A directory of historic locations, 1913–1923*. Dublin: Dublin City Council

Connolly, S. J. (ed.) (1998) *The Oxford Companion to Irish History*. Oxford: Oxford University Press

Coogan, T. P. (1991) *Michael Collins: A Biography*. London: Arrow Books Limited

Cowell, J. (1980) *Where They Lived in Dublin*. Dublin: The O'Brien Press Limited

Cronin, S. (1980) *Frank Ryan: The Search for The Republic*. Dublin: Repsol Publishing

Dublin's Fighting Story, 1916–1921, Told by the Men who Made It.
Cork: Mercier Press 2009

Dwyer, T. Ryle. (2005) *The Squad and the Intelligence Operations of Michael Collins.* Cork: Mercier Press.

Dwyer, T. Ryle. (2006) *'I Signed My Death Warrant': Michael Collins and the Treaty.* Cork: Mercier Press

Fido, M. (1988) *Bodysnatchers: A History of the Resurrectionists.* London: George Weidenfeld & Nicolson Limited

Fisk, R. (1985) *In Time of War: Ireland, Ulster and the price of neutrality 1939-45.* London: Paladin Books

Fleetwood, J. (1988) *The Irish Body Snatchers: A history of body snatching in Ireland.* Dublin: Tomar Publishing Ltd

Foley, C. (1992) *Legion of the Rearguard: The IRA and the Modern Irish State.* London: Pluto Press

Geoghegan, P. M. (2010) *Liberator: The Life and Death of Daniel O'Connell 1830–1847.* Dublin: Gill & Macmillan Ltd

Graves, R. (1998) *Good-bye to All That: An Autobiography.* New York: Anchor Books

Hopkins, F. (2002) *Rare Old Dublin: Heroes, Hawkers and Hoors.* Cork: Mercier Press

Hopkins, F. (2007) *Hidden Dublin: Deadbeats, Dossers and Decent Skins.* Cork: Mercier Press

Henry, Fr OFM Cap. (ed.) (1967) *The Capuchin Annual 1967.* Dublin

Igoe, V. (2001) *Dublin Burial Grounds & Graveyards.* Dublin: Wolfhound Press Ltd

Irish Times (1859–2010) The Irish Times Archive. http://www.irishtimes.com/archive

Jordan, A. J. (1998) *Christy Brown's Women: A biography drawing on his letters.* Dublin: Westport Books

Kearns, K. C. (2000) *Dublin Tenement Life: An Oral History.* London: Penguin Books Ltd

Kerrigan, M. (2007) *The History of Death: Burial customs and funeral rites, from the ancient world to modern times.* London: Amber Books Ltd

Lyons, J. B. (1991) *'What Did I Die Of?': The Deaths of Parnell, Wilde, Synge, and Other Literary Pathologies*. Dublin: The Lilliput Press Ltd

Ni Dheirg, I. (2008) *The Story of Michael Collins* (Irish Heroes for Children Series). Cork: Mercier Press

Macken, U. (2008) *The Story of Daniel O'Connell* (Irish Heroes for Children Series). Cork: Mercier Press

McCoole, S. (2004) *No Ordinary Women: Irish Female Activists in the Revolutionary Years 1900–1923*. Dublin: The O'Brien Press Ltd

McGarry, F. (2002) *Frank Ryan*. Dublin: Historical Association of Ireland

McGarry, F. (2005) *Eoin O'Duffy: A Self-Made Hero*. Oxford: Oxford University Press

McMahon, S. and O'Donoghue, J. (1998) *The Mercier Companion to Irish Literature*. Cork: Mercier Press

MacCiarnáin, S. (1976) *The Last Post*. Dublin: National Graves Association

McMahon, S. (2001) *Rebel Ireland: From Easter Rising to Civil War*. Cork: Mercier Press

MacThomáis, E. (1975) *Me jewel and darlin' Dublin*. Dublin: The O'Brien Press Ltd

MacThomáis, S. (2010) *Glasnevin: Ireland's Necropolis*. Dublin: Glasnevin Trust

Ó Broin, S. (1999) *Inchicore, Kilmainham and District*. Dublin: Cois Camóige Publications

O'Donnell, E. E., SJ (1990) *The Genius of Fr Browne: Ireland's Photographic Discovery*. Dublin: Wolfhound Press

O'Donovan Rossa, J. (2004) *Rossa's Recollections 1838 to 1898: Memoirs of an Irish Revolutionary*. Guilford: The Lyons Press

O'Duffy, R. J. (1915) *Historic Graves in Glasnevin Cemetery*. Dublin: James Duffy and Co. Ltd

O'Farrell, M. (1999) *A Walk through Rebel Dublin 1916*. Cork: Mercier Press

O'Farrell, M. (2009) *50 Things You Didn't Know About 1916.* Cork: Mercier Press

O'Mahony, S. (1987) *Frongoch: University of Revolution.* Dublin: FDR Teoranta

O'Shea, S. (2000) *Death and Design in Victorian Glasnevin.* Dublin: Dublin Cemeteries Committee

O'Sullivan, M. (1997) *Brendan Behan: A Life.* Dublin: Blackwater Press

Robbins, F. (1977) *Under The Starry Plough: Recollections of the Irish Citizen Army.* Dublin: The Academy Press

Silverman, M. (2001) *An Irish Working Class: Explorations in Political Economy and Hegemony, 1800–1950.* Toronto: University of Toronto Press Incorporated

Stradling, R. A. (1999) *The Irish and the Spanish Civil War 1936–1939.* Manchester: Mandolin

Wade, S. (2008) *Foul Deeds and Suspicious Deaths in Dublin.* South Yorkshire: Wharncliffe Books

Yeates, P. (2001) *Lockout Dublin 1913.* Dublin: Gill & Macmillan

∻ ACKNOWLEDGEMENTS ∻

The graveyards of Dublin tell a story of the city we now live in. Sometimes it is a story of a greatness performed, but other times it reflects a life lived boldly in obscurity.

This book would simply have not been possible without the assistance of many people.

I would like to thank the Glasnevin Trust, who employ me in one of the most interesting jobs in Ireland. Dr Peter Harbison, who corrected my faulty prose and punctuation. The members of Glasnevin Trust Curatorial Committee, in particular, its chairperson Jonathan Bailey. George McCullough, CEO Glasnevin Trust, who encouraged me to write this book. Alison Crinion, who manages my unmanageability, and all of the staff of Glasnevin Trust, in particular Dave Thompson, who has the misfortune of sharing an office with me, and Graham Donnelly, who decides what is merely 'interesting', as opposed to 'dead interesting'.

Laura Murtagh of Martello Media, whose brilliant writing for the Glasnevin Museum Milestone Gallery I continually return to plunder for fact and detail. Laz Fallon of the Fireman's Museum, who is an encyclopaedia of knowledge. Lorcan Collins of the 1916 Rising Tour, who first suggested writing this book. The staff of the National Library of Ireland, The National Photographic Archive and The National Archives, Kew, whose professionalism was a byword.

I have included a bibliography, but two writers deserve mention here, Ray Bateson and Vivien Igoe, both rich veins of information on the cemeteries of Dublin. A special thanks to Conor Dodd who explained many a military term and supplied me with countless images. The staff of Mercier Press, who turned a badly edited document into the book you are now holding.

On a personal level, I would like to thank my father, Éamonn, whose voice I still hear. My friends, Conor and Jack, who always believed in me. Morgane, my beautiful daughter who inspired me to live. And lastly, but most importantly, Ruth, my partner, who edits everything I do and without whom I would truly be lost.

Shane MacThomáis